Steve Burggraf, Guillaume Pagliano, Alexandre Auriac & Elsa Launay

Hot Dogs
HAMBURGERS
TACOS AND
margaritas

Smith
Street
Books

Table of Contents

SAUSAGE Secrets

Take your pick

With so many sausage styles available, you can have great fun experimenting and being creative with your hot dog inventions. Here are some of the main sausage varieties you'll come across these days.

STRASBOURG OR KNACKWURST

– a smoked pork sausage, recognisable by its dark pink skin.

FRANKFURT

– a smoked sausage, usually an orange colour, and usually made from pure pork, but sometimes also beef or veal.

VIENNA

– made from a mix of veal and pork, and usually pale orange in colour.

CHIPOLATA

– made from pork, and often seasoned with herbs such as thyme or sage, or spices such as nutmeg.

All of these are great choices for hot dogs, each differing slightly in colour, texture and taste.

Quality is key

The secret to a great hot dog is to start with a good-quality sausage from a butcher or delicatessen.

The sausages you buy for hot dogs are generally pre-cooked, and just need to be warmed for serving; the way in which they are initially cooked will determine their quality. Basically, there are two types of pre-cooked sausages commercially available: those cooked in a steam oven, and those cooked by immersion in boiling water. The second method produces the tastiest sausage.

The quality of the casing is also fundamental. Make sure it is 'natural', rather than being made of collagen, as the sausage will have better texture when bitten into.

Banish the microwave

Never, ever heat a sausage in the microwave, because it will dry out. Instead, bring a large saucepan of water to the boil, turn off the heat, add the sausage and leave to warm through for 5–6 minutes. Keep an eye on the sausage, though, because the skin can split if you leave it too long.

You can also cook your sausages on a grill.

GETTING
Saucy

Once you've got your sausages sorted, it's time to flavour up with a good squeeze of ketchup and mustard, and perhaps a dollop of relish.

Must-have mustard!

A hot dog isn't a hot dog without mustard – whether it's a smear of yellow American, hot English, dijon, wholegrain, or even a fruit mustard.

You can pep things up even further by adding some extra flavour elements to your favourite mustard – for starters, try out the ideas to the right. Each mustard makes enough for 4 hot dogs.

BASIL MUSTARD

Mix together 1 chopped garlic clove, 4 finely shredded basil leaves and 200 g (7 oz) dijon or wholegrain mustard.

GINGER MUSTARD

Mix together 1 tablespoon very finely chopped fresh ginger, 1 tablespoon lemon juice and 200 g (7 oz) dijon or wholegrain mustard.

CHILLI MUSTARD

Fry 1–2 small red chillies in 1 tablespoon sunflower oil. Crush to a purée, then mix through 200 g (7 oz) dijon mustard.

HONEY MUSTARD

In a small saucepan, over low heat, mix together 200 g (7 oz) crème fraîche, 2 tablespoons mustard (wholegrain is good), 2 tablespoons honey and 2 teaspoons soy sauce. Simmer for 5 minutes, stirring regularly.

Classic ketchup
FOR 8 HOT DOGS

80 ml (2½ fl oz/⅓ cup) olive oil

2 kg (4 lb 6 oz) ripe tomatoes, cut into quarters

500 g (1 lb 2 oz) red capsicums (bell peppers), chopped

500 g (1 lb 2 oz) onions, sliced

100 g (3½ oz) sugar

250 ml (8½ fl oz/1 cup) balsamic vinegar

2 tablespoons hot mustard

1 teaspoon salt

½ teaspoon freshly grated nutmeg

1 teaspoon smoked paprika

½ teaspoon chilli powder

Heat the oil in a heavy-based saucepan over medium heat. Add the vegetables and cook for 45 minutes, stirring often, until nicely browned. Leave to cool slightly.

Blitz in a food processor, then return to the pan and stir in the sugar, vinegar, mustard, salt and spices and 250 ml (8½ fl oz/1 cup) water. Simmer over low heat for 40 minutes, stirring occasionally, and adding a little water if needed.

Season to taste with salt and pepper and strain through a fine-mesh sieve. Store in a clean squeeze-bottle in the fridge.

Gherkin relish
FOR 4 HOT DOGS

8 large gherkins (pickles), chopped

1 tablespoon acacia honey

1 teaspoon curry powder

1 teaspoon ground ginger

Chop the gherkins and place in a small bowl. Add the remaining ingredients and mix until combined. Season to taste with salt and pepper.

Topping it off

Sure, you can stick to the simple combo of sausage + ketchup + mustard – or you can spice things up by adding some toppings for extra texture, crunch and flavour.

Try capers, caramelised onion, raw red onion, chopped olives, tomatoes, a sprinkling of spices such as sumac or pepper, fresh herbs such as chives, basil and coriander (cilantro), horseradish cream, guacamole, chutney, relishes such as piccalilli, chopped grapes, raisins or prunes, and even crushed nuts such as hazelnuts, walnuts or pine nuts…

There are three basic rules to follow for the perfectly topped hot dog.

Don't go overboard!

Limit the number of toppings to a maximum of five, or you'll risk sensory overload.

Play with textures

Your palate will appreciate even more the softness of the bread and the gooey-ness of melting cheese if these are punctuated with a few surprises like crunchy walnuts, hazelnuts, peanuts or crispy fried shallots.

Balance the flavours

Remember to offset the acidity of a cheese with a sweet topping. The classic example is the combination of a tangy blue cheese and sweet caramelised onion.

Hot tip!

For all ingredients that do not require cooking, bring them to room temperature before using, to keep the hot dog as warm and tasty as possible.

Brilliant
HOT DOG BUNS

20 g (¾ oz) fresh yeast

120–150 ml (4–5 fl oz) lukewarm milk

430 g (15 oz) plain (all-purpose) flour

1 teaspoon salt

1 tablespoon sugar

1 egg, lightly beaten with 1 egg yolk

1 tablespoon melted butter

sesame seeds or poppy seeds, for sprinkling (optional)

In a small bowl, stir together the yeast and 120 ml (4 fl oz) milk. Set aside for a few minutes.

In a large bowl, combine the flour, salt and sugar, then make a well in the centre. Pour in the eggs, butter and the milk and yeast mixture.

Combine using your hands, working the flour into the centre. If the dough is too dry, add a little more milk, until you have a fairly soft ball that detaches from the bowl. Tip the dough ball onto a lightly floured surface and knead for 10 minutes, until the consistency is smooth and elastic. Reshape into a ball, cover with a damp tea towel and leave to rise in a warm place for 1 hour.

Knock the air out of the dough, then divide into six portions of about 120 g (4½ oz) each. Cover again and rest for another 5 minutes.

Shape the dough into mini baguette shapes about 10 cm (4 in) long.

Place the hot dog rolls on a baking tray lined with baking paper, leaving a good amount of space in between them as they will expand during cooking. Cover with a damp tea towel and leave to rise again for 45 minutes.

Preheat the oven to 180°C (350°F).

If you like, sprinkle the bread with your favourite seeds. Bake for 10–15 minutes, until the buns are golden brown and sound hollow when tapped underneath.

Leave to cool on a wire rack. Any buns that aren't needed within a day or two can be frozen for later use.

Cheese & pickle DOG

1 x 60 g (2 oz) knackwurst sausage

1 hot dog bun (page 15)

1–2 tablespoons cream cheese

1 tablespoon Gherkin relish (page 11)

1 tablespoon crispy fried shallots

2 teaspoons Ginger mustard (page 11)

2 teaspoons Classic ketchup (page 11)

Preheat the oven to 160°C (320°F).

Bring a saucepan of water to the boil, then turn off the heat. Add the sausage and leave to heat through for 5–6 minutes, being sure to remove it from the water before it splits. Drain briefly.

Meanwhile, cut the hot dog bun in half and wrap in foil. Place on the middle shelf in the oven and bake for 3 minutes.

To assemble, spread the cream cheese on the bottom half of the bun. Follow with the relish and fried shallots. Add the sausage and top with the mustard and ketchup. Put the bun lid on top and serve immediately.

1 x 60 g (2 oz) chicken
sausage

1 hot dog bun (page 15)

1–2 tablespoons cream cheese

1 tablespoon crispy fried shallots

2 teaspoons Honey mustard
(page 11)

2 teaspoons Classic ketchup
(page 11)

Preheat the oven to 160°C (320°F).

Bring a saucepan of water to the boil, then turn off the heat. Add the sausage and leave to heat through for 5–6 minutes, being sure to remove it from the water before it splits. Drain briefly.

Meanwhile, cut the hot dog bun in half and wrap in foil. Place on the middle shelf in the oven and bake for 3 minutes.

To assemble, spread the cream cheese on the bottom half of the bun. Follow with the fried shallots, then add the sausage. Top with the mustard and ketchup. Put the bun lid on top and serve immediately.

Blue cheese dog
WITH CARAMELISED ONION

1 tablespoon butter

½ onion, sliced

1 x 60 g (2 oz) knackwurst sausage

1 hot dog bun (page 15)

30 g (1 oz/¼ cup) roughly crumbled blue cheese

2 teaspoons Honey mustard (page 11)

2 teaspoons Classic ketchup (page 11)

Preheat the oven to 160°C (320°F).

Melt the butter in a frying pan over medium heat. Add the onion and cook for about 1 minute, until starting to soften. Reduce the heat to low and cook for another 7 minutes, or until the onion is soft and caramelised. Keep warm.

Bring a saucepan of water to the boil, then turn off the heat. Add the sausage and leave to heat through for 5–6 minutes, being sure to remove it from the water before it splits. Drain briefly.

Meanwhile, cut the hot dog bun in half and wrap in foil. Place on the middle shelf in the oven and bake for 3 minutes.

Warm the blue cheese in a small saucepan over low heat for 2–3 minutes, until just melted.

To assemble, spread the melted cheese on the bottom half of the bun. Follow with the caramelised onions, then add the sausage. Top with the mustard and ketchup. Put the bun lid on top and serve immediately.

The Z-dog

2 tablespoons olive oil

juice of ½ lemon

¼ zucchini (courgette), thinly sliced

1 x 60 g (2 oz) Vienna sausage

1 hot dog bun (page 15)

30 g (1 oz/¼ cup) roughly crumbled goat's cheese

2 tablespoons chopped toasted hazelnuts

2 teaspoons grape-must mustard

Combine the olive oil and lemon juice in a small bowl. Add the zucchini slices and leave to marinate for 15 minutes.

Heat a frying pan over medium heat and sauté the zucchini for 4–5 minutes. Keep warm.

Meanwhile, preheat the oven to 160°C (320°F).

Bring a saucepan of water to the boil, then turn off the heat. Add the sausage and leave to heat through for 5–6 minutes, being sure to remove it from the water before it splits. Drain briefly.

While the sausage is warming, cut the hot dog bun in half and wrap in foil. Place on the middle shelf in the oven and bake for 3 minutes.

Warm the goat's cheese in a small saucepan over low heat for 2–3 minutes, until just melted.

To assemble, spread the melted cheese on the bottom half of the bun. Follow with the crushed hazelnuts and the zucchini. Add the sausage and top with the mustard. Put the bun lid on top and serve immediately.

YEAH-YEAH
gruyère dog

1 x 60 g (2 oz) Vienna sausage

1 hot dog bun (page 15)

30 g (1 oz/¼ cup) roughly crumbled gruyère

3 semi-dried (sun-blushed) tomatoes, chopped

3 black olives, pitted and chopped

2 teaspoons yellow American mustard

Preheat the oven to 160°C (320°F).

Bring a saucepan of water to the boil, then turn off the heat. Add the sausage and leave to heat through for 5–6 minutes, being sure to remove it from the water before it splits. Drain briefly.

Meanwhile, cut the hot dog bun in half and wrap in foil. Place on the middle shelf in the oven and bake for 3 minutes.

Warm the cheese in a small saucepan over low heat for 2–3 minutes, until just melted.

To assemble, spread the melted cheese on the bottom half of the bun. Follow with the tomatoes and olives. Add the sausage and top with the mustard. Put the bun lid on top and serve immediately.

Ooh-la-la FRENCHIE DOG

2 tablespoons olive oil

zest and juice of ½ lemon

¼ eggplant (aubergine), thinly sliced

1 x 60 g (2 oz) chicken sausage

1 hot dog bun (page 15)

30 g (1 oz/¼ cup) roughly crumbled brie or camembert

2 teaspoons Honey mustard (page 11)

Combine the olive oil, lemon zest and lemon juice in a small bowl. Add the eggplant slices and leave to marinate for 15 minutes.

Heat a frying pan over medium heat and sauté the eggplant for 4–5 minutes. Keep warm.

Meanwhile, preheat the oven to 160°C (320°F).

Bring a saucepan of water to the boil, then turn off the heat. Add the sausage and leave to heat through for 5–6 minutes, being sure to remove it from the water before it splits. Drain briefly.

While the sausage is warming, cut the hot dog bun in half and wrap in foil. Place on the middle shelf in the oven and bake for 3 minutes.

Warm the cheese in a small saucepan over low heat for 2–3 minutes, until just melted.

To assemble, spread the eggplant slices on the bottom half of the bun. Follow with the melted cheese. Add the sausage and top with the mustard. Put the bun lid on top and serve immediately.

Cheesy dog WITH WALNUTS

1 x 60 g (2 oz) knackwurst sausage

1 hot dog bun (page 15)

30 g (1 oz/¼ cup) roughly chopped cumin-spiced gouda

2 tablespoons chopped walnuts

2 teaspoons Ginger mustard (page 11)

Preheat the oven to 160°C (320ºF).

Bring a saucepan of water to the boil, then turn off the heat. Add the sausage and leave to heat through for 5–6 minutes, being sure to remove it from the water before it splits. Drain briefly.

Meanwhile, cut the hot dog bun in half and wrap in foil. Place on the middle shelf in the oven and bake for 3 minutes.

Warm the cheese in a small saucepan over low heat for 2–3 minutes, until just melted.

To assemble, spread the melted cheese on the bottom half of the bun. Follow with the walnuts. Add the sausage and top with the mustard. Put the bun lid on top and serve immediately.

Smoky DOG

1 x 60 g (2 oz) Vienna sausage

1 hot dog bun (page 15)

30 g (1 oz/¼ cup) roughly crumbled ash-coated goat's cheese

1–2 tablespoons baba ghanoush

2 teaspoons Honey mustard (page 11)

Preheat the oven to 160°C (320°F).

Bring a saucepan of water to the boil, then turn off the heat. Add the sausage and leave to heat through for 5–6 minutes, being sure to remove it from the water before it splits. Drain briefly.

Meanwhile, cut the hot dog bun in half and wrap in foil. Place on the middle shelf in the oven and bake for 3 minutes.

Warm the cheese in a small saucepan over low heat for 2–3 minutes, until just melted.

To assemble, spread the baba ghanoush on the bottom half of the bun. Follow with the melted cheese. Add the sausage and top with the mustard. Put the bun lid on top and serve immediately.

Turnin' the beet around DOG

1 x 60 g (2 oz) knackwurst sausage

1 hot dog bun (page 15)

1–2 tablespoons cream cheese

2 tablespoons diced cooked beetroot (beet)

2 teaspoons hot wholegrain mustard

Preheat the oven to 160°C (320°F).

Bring a saucepan of water to the boil, then turn off the heat. Add the sausage and leave to heat through for 5–6 minutes, being sure to remove it from the water before it splits. Drain briefly.

Meanwhile, cut the hot dog bun in half and wrap in foil. Place on the middle shelf in the oven and bake for 3 minutes.

To assemble, spread the cream cheese on the bottom half of the bun. Follow with the beetroot, then top with the sausage and mustard. Put the bun lid on top and serve immediately.

Hazel dog

1 x 60 g (2 oz) knackwurst sausage

1 hot dog bun (page 15)

30 g (1 oz/¼ cup) roughly chopped camembert or brie

2 teaspoons barbecue sauce

2 tablespoons chopped hazelnuts

Preheat the oven to 160°C (320°F).

Bring a saucepan of water to the boil, then turn off the heat. Add the sausage and leave to heat through for 5–6 minutes, being sure to remove it from the water before it splits. Drain briefly.

Meanwhile, cut the hot dog bun in half and wrap in foil. Place on the middle shelf in the oven and bake for 3 minutes.

Warm the cheese in a small saucepan over low heat for 2–3 minutes, until just melted.

To assemble, spread the melted cheese on the bottom half of the bun. Top with the sausage, then the barbecue sauce. Sprinkle with the hazelnuts. Put the bun lid on top and serve immediately.

Spicy mustard dog
WITH RED ONION

1 x 60 g (2 oz) knackwurst sausage

1 hot dog bun (page 15)

30 g (1 oz/¼ cup) roughly chopped brie or camembert

¼ red onion, thinly sliced

2 teaspoons spiced mustard

Preheat the oven to 160°C (320°F).

Bring a saucepan of water to the boil, then turn off the heat. Add the sausage and leave to heat through for 5–6 minutes, being sure to remove it from the water before it splits. Drain briefly.

Meanwhile, cut the hot dog bun in half and wrap in foil. Place on the middle shelf in the oven and bake for 3 minutes.

Warm the cheese in a small saucepan over low heat for 2–3 minutes, until just melted.

To assemble, spread the melted cheese on the bottom half of the bun. Top with the onion slices. Add the sausage and top with the spiced mustard. Put the bun lid on top and serve immediately.

Olive dog

1 x 60 g (2 oz) knackwurst sausage

1 hot dog bun (page 15)

1 tablespoon olive tapenade

2 teaspoons Classic ketchup (page 11)

2 teaspoons Ginger mustard (page 11)

30 g (1 oz/¼ cup) shaved parmesan

Preheat the oven to 160°C (320°F).

Bring a saucepan of water to the boil, then turn off the heat. Add the sausage and leave to heat through for 5–6 minutes, being sure to remove it from the water before it splits. Drain briefly.

Meanwhile, cut the hot dog bun in half and wrap in foil. Place on the middle shelf in the oven and bake for 3 minutes.

To assemble, spread the tapenade on the bottom half of the bun. Add the sausage and top with the ketchup and mustard. Follow with the parmesan. Put the bun lid on top and serve immediately.

Herby artichoke DOG

1 x 60 g (2 oz) knackwurst sausage

1 hot dog bun (page 15)

1–2 tablespoons herbed cream cheese

3 marinated artichoke hearts, sliced

2 teaspoons wholegrain mustard

2 teaspoons Classic ketchup (page 11)

Preheat the oven to 160°C (320°F).

Bring a saucepan of water to the boil, then turn off the heat. Add the sausage and leave to heat through for 5–6 minutes, being sure to remove it from the water before it splits. Drain briefly.

Meanwhile, cut the hot dog bun in half and wrap in foil. Place on the middle shelf in the oven and bake for 3 minutes.

To assemble, spread the cream cheese on the bottom half of the bun. Top with the artichoke, then the sausage, mustard and ketchup. Put the bun lid on top and serve immediately.

The caper DOG

1 x 60 g (2 oz) knackwurst sausage

1 hot dog bun (page 15)

30 g (1 oz/¼ cup) roughly chopped Swiss cheese

1 tablespoon pine nuts

1–2 tablespoons capers

2 teaspoons Classic ketchup (page 11)

Preheat the oven to 160°C (320°F).

Bring a saucepan of water to the boil, then turn off the heat. Add the sausage and leave to heat through for 5–6 minutes, being sure to remove it from the water before it splits. Drain briefly.

Meanwhile, cut the hot dog bun in half and wrap in foil. Place on the middle shelf in the oven and bake for 3 minutes.

Warm the cheese in a small saucepan over low heat for 2–3 minutes, until just melted.

To assemble, spread the melted cheese on the bottom half of the bun. Follow with the pine nuts and capers. Add the sausage and top with the ketchup. Put the bun lid on top and serve immediately.

The Kremlin DOG

1 x 60 g (2 oz) Vienna sausage

1 hot dog bun (page 15)

2 prunes, pitted and chopped

2 teaspoons wholegrain mustard

2 teaspoons Classic ketchup (page 11)

PICKLED RED CABBAGE

25 g (1 oz/⅓ cup) shredded red cabbage

½ teaspoon salt

100 ml (3½ fl oz) vinegar

2–3 peppercorns

1–2 cloves

Start pickling the cabbage 3 days in advance. Place in a small non-metallic dish and sprinkle with the salt. Place a weight (such as a small plate with a tin of food on top) over the cabbage to keep it pressed down. Leave in the fridge for 3 days, then drain.

In a small saucepan, bring the vinegar, peppercorns and cloves to the boil. Leave to simmer for a few minutes, to reduce and thicken slightly, then remove the spices and mix the vinegar through the cabbage. Set aside.

Preheat the oven to 160°C (320°F).

Bring a saucepan of water to the boil, then turn off the heat. Add the sausage and leave to heat through for 5–6 minutes, being sure to remove it from the water before it splits. Drain briefly.

Meanwhile, cut the hot dog bun in half and wrap in foil. Place on the middle shelf in the oven and bake for 3 minutes.

To assemble, place the pickled cabbage and prunes on the bottom half of the bun. Add the sausage, then top with the mustard and ketchup. Put the bun lid on top and serve immediately.

The German DOG

1 x 60 g (2 oz) Vienna sausage

1 hot dog bun (page 15)

30 g (1 oz/¼ cup) roughly crumbled gruyère

2 tablespoons sauerkraut

1 tablespoon crispy fried shallots

2 teaspoons grape-must mustard

Preheat the oven to 160°C (320°F).

Bring a saucepan of water to the boil, then turn off the heat. Add the sausage and leave to heat through for 5–6 minutes, being sure to remove it from the water before it splits. Drain briefly.

Meanwhile, cut the hot dog bun in half and wrap in foil. Place on the middle shelf in the oven and bake for 3 minutes.

Warm the cheese in a small saucepan over low heat for 2–3 minutes, until just melted.

To assemble, spread the melted cheese on the bottom half of the bun. Follow with the sauerkraut and fried shallots. Add the sausage and top with the mustard. Put the bun lid on top and serve immediately.

Bacon & raclette DOG

1 x 60 g (2 oz) knackwurst sausage

1–2 bacon rashers (slices)

1 hot dog bun (page 15)

30 g (1 oz/¼ cup) roughly chopped raclette or fontina

2 tablespoons spiced mustard

Preheat the oven to 160°C (320°F).

Bring a saucepan of water to the boil, then turn off the heat. Add the sausage and leave to heat through for 5–6 minutes, being sure to remove it from the water before it splits. Drain briefly.

Meanwhile, cook the bacon for about 5 minutes in a frying pan without any oil. Keep warm.

Cut the hot dog bun in half and wrap in foil. Place on the middle shelf in the oven and bake for 3 minutes.

Warm the cheese in a small saucepan over low heat for 2–3 minutes, until just melted.

To assemble, spread the melted cheese on the bottom half of the bun. Add the sausage and bacon, then top with the mustard. Put the bun lid on top and serve immediately.

Poutine DOG

½ potato

2 tablespoons sunflower oil

a pinch of ground cumin

1 x 60 g (2 oz) knackwurst sausage

1 hot dog bun (page 15)

30 g (1 oz/¼ cup) roughly chopped cheddar or monterey jack

2 teaspoons Classic ketchup (page 11)

2 teaspoons wholegrain mustard

Preheat the oven to 160°C (320°F).

Peel and grate the potato, squeezing out any excess liquid. Heat the oil in a frying pan over low heat. Add the potato, sprinkle with the cumin and cook for 6–7 minutes. Keep warm.

Meanwhile, bring a saucepan of water to the boil, then turn off the heat. Add the sausage and leave to heat through for 5–6 minutes, being sure to remove it from the water before it splits. Drain briefly.

Cut the hot dog bun in half and wrap in foil. Place on the middle shelf in the oven and bake for 3 minutes.

Warm the cheese in a small saucepan over low heat for 2–3 minutes, until just melted.

To assemble, spread the melted cheese on the bottom half of the bun. Top with the potato. Add the sausage, then top with the ketchup and mustard. Put the bun lid on top and serve immediately.

Chicken dog
WITH BACON

1 x 60 g (2 oz) chicken sausage

1 bacon rasher (slice), chopped

a few drops of balsamic vinegar

1 hot dog bun (page 15)

30 g (1 oz/¼ cup) roughly chopped camembert or brie

2 teaspoons wholegrain mustard

2 teaspoons Classic ketchup (page 11)

Preheat the oven to 160°C (320°F).

Bring a saucepan of water to the boil, then turn off the heat. Add the sausage and leave to heat through for 5–6 minutes, being sure to remove it from the water before it splits. Drain briefly.

Meanwhile, cook the bacon with the balsamic vinegar in a frying pan over medium heat for 4–5 minutes. Keep warm.

Cut the hot dog bun in half and wrap in foil. Place on the middle shelf in the oven and bake for 3 minutes.

Warm the cheese in a small saucepan over low heat for 2–3 minutes, until just melted.

To assemble, spread the melted cheese on the bottom half of the bun. Sprinkle with the chopped bacon. Add the sausage, then top with the mustard and ketchup. Put the bun lid on top and serve immediately.

Cheese 'n' onion DOG

MAKES 1

1 tablespoon butter

½ onion, sliced

1 x 60 g (2 oz) knackwurst sausage

1 hot dog bun (page 15)

30 g (1 oz/¼ cup) roughly chopped sharp cheddar

2 teaspoons Chilli mustard (page 11)

Preheat the oven to 160°C (320ºF).

Melt the butter in a frying pan over medium heat. Add the onion and cook for about 1 minute, until starting to soften. Reduce the heat to low and cook for another 7 minutes, or until the onion is soft and caramelised. Keep warm.

Meanwhile, bring a saucepan of water to the boil, then turn off the heat. Add the sausage and leave to heat through for 5–6 minutes, being sure to remove it from the water before it splits. Drain briefly.

Cut the hot dog bun in half and wrap in foil. Place on the middle shelf in the oven and bake for 3 minutes.

Warm the cheese in a small saucepan over low heat for 2–3 minutes, until just melted.

To assemble, spread the caramelised onion and melted cheese on the bottom half of the bun. Add the sausage, then top with the mustard. Put the bun lid on top and serve immediately.

Black pud & apple DOG

1½ tablespoons butter

¼ apple, peeled and diced

1 x 60 g (2 oz) black pudding sausage

1 hot dog bun (page 15)

2 teaspoons Honey mustard (page 11)

Preheat the oven to 160°C (320°F).

Melt the butter in a frying pan over low heat. Add the apple and cook for 5–6 minutes. Keep warm.

Meanwhile, in another frying pan, fry the sausage for 4–5 minutes, or until cooked through. Season with salt and pepper.

Cut the hot dog bun in half and wrap in foil. Place on the middle shelf in the oven and bake for 3 minutes.

To assemble, spread half the apple over the bottom half of the bun. Add the sausage, then top with the mustard and the remaining apple. Put the bun lid on top and serve immediately.

Wine & cheese DOG

MAKES 1

1 x 60 g (2 oz) Vienna sausage

1 hot dog bun (page 15)

30 g (1 oz/¼ cup) roughly chopped camembert or brie

2 teaspoons grape-must mustard

Preheat the oven to 160°C (320°F).

Bring a saucepan of water to the boil, then turn off the heat. Add the sausage and leave to heat through for 5–6 minutes, being sure to remove it from the water before it splits. Drain briefly.

Meanwhile, cut the hot dog bun in half and wrap in foil. Place on the middle shelf in the oven and bake for 3 minutes.

Warm the cheese in a small saucepan over low heat for 2–3 minutes, until just melted.

To assemble, spread the melted cheese over the bottom half of the bun. Add the sausage, then top with the mustard. Put the bun lid on top and serve immediately.

Hot chilli DOG

1 x 60 g (2 oz) knackwurst sausage

1 hot dog bun (page 15)

1–2 tablespoons cream cheese

1–2 tablespoons Gherkin relish (page 11)

1 tablespoon crispy fried shallots

2 teaspoons Chilli mustard (page 11)

3–4 drops Tabasco or other hot chilli sauce

Preheat the oven to 160°C (320°F).

Bring a saucepan of water to the boil, then turn off the heat. Add the sausage and leave to heat through for 5–6 minutes, being sure to remove it from the water before it splits. Drain briefly.

Meanwhile, cut the hot dog bun in half and wrap in foil. Place on the middle shelf in the oven and bake for 3 minutes.

To assemble, spread the cream cheese on the bottom half of the bun. Follow with the relish and fried shallots. Add the sausage, then top with the chilli mustard and a few drops of hot sauce. Put the bun lid on top and serve immediately.

Lil' dog
WITH
LEMONY PEPPERS

2 x 30 g (1 oz) chipolata sausages

2 tablespoons olive oil

¼ capsicum (bell pepper), cut into strips

zest and juice of ½ lemon

1 hot dog bun (page 15)

2 teaspoons Chilli mustard (page 11)

Preheat the oven to 160°C (320°F).

Bring a saucepan of water to the boil, then turn off the heat. Add the sausages and leave to heat through for 5–6 minutes, being sure to remove them from the water before they split. Drain briefly.

Meanwhile, heat the oil in a frying pan over medium heat. Add the capsicum, lemon zest and lemon juice and cook for 4–5 minutes, until tender.

Cut the hot dog bun in half and wrap in foil. Place on the middle shelf in the oven and cook for 3 minutes.

To assemble, place the capsicum on the bottom half of the bun. Add the sausages, then top with the mustard. Put the bun lid on top and serve immediately.

Slaw DOG

1 x 60 g (2 oz) knackwurst sausage

1 hot dog bun (page 15)

2 tablespoons Coleslaw (page 89)

1–2 tablespoons sultanas (golden raisins)

2 teaspoons Classic ketchup (page 11)

Preheat the oven to 160°C (320°F).

Bring a saucepan of water to the boil, then turn off the heat. Add the sausage and leave to heat through for 5–6 minutes, being sure to remove it from the water before it splits. Drain briefly.

Meanwhile, cut the hot dog bun in half and wrap in foil. Place on the middle shelf in the oven and bake for 3 minutes.

To assemble, spread the coleslaw over the bottom half of the bun and sprinkle with the sultanas. Add the sausage then top with the ketchup. Put the bun lid on top and serve immediately.

The Italian DOG

1 x 60 g (2 oz) Vienna sausage

1 hot dog bun (page 15)

30 g (1 oz/¼ cup) sliced fresh mozzarella

4 semi-dried (sun-blushed) tomatoes, sliced

2 teaspoons Basil mustard (page 11)

2 teaspoons Classic ketchup (page 11)

Preheat the oven to 160°C (320°F).

Bring a saucepan of water to the boil, then turn off the heat. Add the sausage and leave to heat through for 5–6 minutes, being sure to remove it from the water before it splits. Drain briefly.

Meanwhile, cut the hot dog bun in half and wrap in foil. Place on the middle shelf in the oven and bake for 3 minutes.

To assemble, place the cheese on the bottom half of the bun. Arrange the tomato slices on top. Add the sausage, then top with the mustard and ketchup. Put the bun lid on top and serve immediately.

The piccalilli circus DOG

1 x 60 g (2 oz) Vienna sausage
1 hot dog bun (page 15)
1–2 tablespoons cream cheese
1 tablespoon crispy fried shallots
2 teaspoons piccalilli relish

Preheat the oven to 160°C (320°F).

Bring a saucepan of water to the boil, then turn off the heat. Add the sausage and leave to heat through for 5–6 minutes, being sure to remove it from the water before it splits. Drain briefly.

Meanwhile, cut the hot dog bun in half and wrap in foil. Place on the middle shelf in the oven and bake for 3 minutes.

To assemble, spread the cream cheese on the bottom half of the bun. Sprinkle with the fried shallots. Add the sausage, then top with the piccalilli. Put the bun lid on top and serve immediately.

The guac DOG

1 x 60 g (2 oz) knackwurst sausage

1 hot dog bun (page 15)

30 g (1 oz/¼ cup) roughly chopped emmental or Swiss cheese

1–2 tablespoons guacamole

2 teaspoons wholegrain mustard

2 teaspoons Classic ketchup (page 11)

Preheat the oven to 160°C (320°F).

Bring a saucepan of water to the boil, then turn off the heat. Add the sausage and leave to heat through for 5–6 minutes, being sure to remove it from the water before it splits. Drain briefly.

Meanwhile, cut the hot dog bun in half and wrap in foil. Place on the middle shelf in the oven and bake for 3 minutes.

Warm the cheese in a small saucepan over low heat for 2–3 minutes, until just melted.

To assemble, spread the guacamole on the bottom half of the bun. Add the sausage, then top with the melted cheese, mustard and ketchup. Put the bun lid on top and serve immediately.

Chicken & chutney DOG

1 x 60 g (2 oz) chicken sausage

1 hot dog bun (page 15)

30 g (1 oz/¼ cup) roughly chopped stilton, or other strong blue cheese

2 teaspoons mango chutney

2 teaspoons wholegrain mustard

Preheat the oven to 160°C (320°F).

Bring a saucepan of water to the boil, then turn off the heat. Add the sausage and leave to heat through for 5–6 minutes, being sure to remove it from the water before it splits. Drain briefly.

Meanwhile, cut the hot dog bun in half and wrap in foil. Place on the middle shelf in the oven and bake for 3 minutes.

Warm the cheese in a small saucepan over low heat for 2–3 minutes, until just melted.

To assemble, spread the melted cheese on the bottom half of the bun. Follow with the chutney. Add the sausage, then top with the mustard. Put the bun lid on top and serve immediately.

CREATING
sensational burgers

ALL ABOUT THE MEAT

When making patties for your burgers, it all starts with the meat, which usually needs to be minced (ground). Here you basically have three options: you can buy your chosen variety of meat already minced, get your butcher to mince it for you, or do it yourself, using a mincer (grinder) or a very sharp knife.

If mincing the meat yourself, ask your butcher for the tastiest and most suitable cuts.

If buying the meat already minced, make sure it is not too lean – it should have a decent amount of fat, so your patties don't dry out too much during cooking.

For the finest texture and flavour, always buy the best quality you can – organic, free-range, grass-fed and pasture-raised whenever possible.

PLAY WITH FLAVOURS!

Don't be afraid to experiment with different flavour elements, to tailor your patties to your own taste.

When mixing your patties, you can incorporate flavoursome additions such as crushed garlic, chopped onion or shallot; spices; chopped herbs such as parsley, coriander (cilantro), chives; thinly sliced vegetables; capers or pickles; tomato paste (concentrated purée), ketchup, soy sauce, wasabi…

These additions will also help bind the meat, so the patties don't fall apart during cooking. Chilling the mixture for 1–2 hours in the fridge before grilling will also help the patties hold together, especially if you're using minced (ground) veal.

If you like, you can also crumb the patties by dipping them in beaten egg and then breadcrumbs before cooking them.

SHAPING THE PATTIES

If you make patties regularly, it's worth considering a simple little hamburger press, which you can buy inexpensively from specialty kitchen shops. The press serves as a mould for the patties, giving a beautifully uniform thickness. Just place 150 g (5½ oz) of the burger mixture into the press and mould it into a patty by pressing the lid down lightly. Be careful not to compress the mixture too much; you don't want to squash all the air out. If it sticks, slide the blade of a knife between the patty and the press.

Alternatively, you can always shape the patties by hand. Form 150 g (5½ oz) portions of the mixture into balls, then gently flatten them to a thickness of about 1.5 cm (½ in).

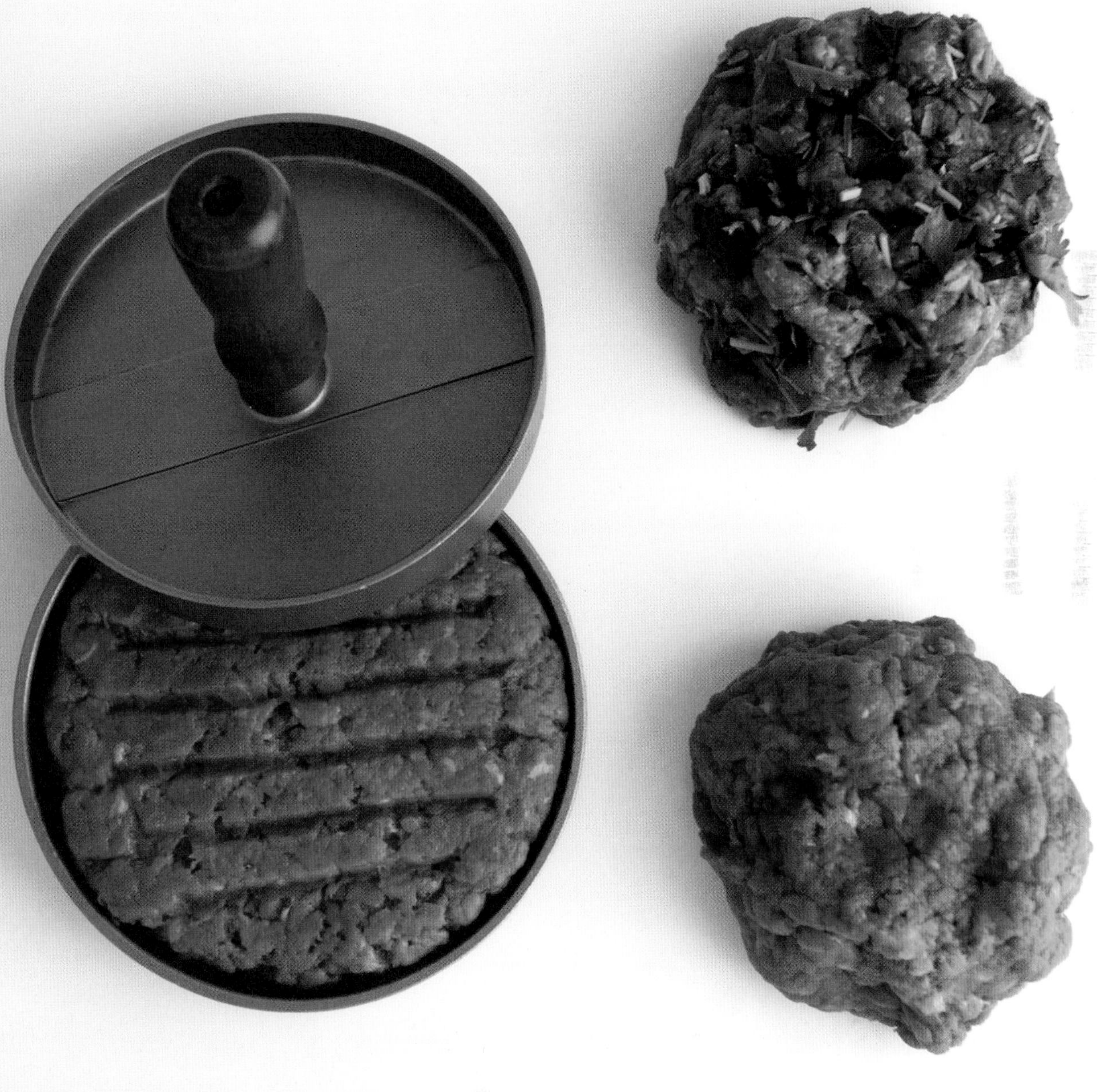

Mastering
THE GRILL

EQUIPMENT

A griddle or chargrill pan is ideal for cooking patties, although a frying pan is also quite suitable. The recipes in this book all use a frying pan.

You won't need to use any oil or fat when cooking on a griddle or non-stick surface, but if cooking in a frying pan, add a few drops of sunflower or vegetable oil first.

A metal spatula will allow you to turn the patties easily; take care if using one on a cooking surface with a non-stick coating.

STEP 1: TURN UP THE HEAT

The first thing you need to do is preheat your griddle or pan for several minutes in advance. The griddle or pan must be very hot the moment you place the patty on. This is what will give the patty a 'crust' on the outside, while maintaining a tender, juicy interior.

Then, do not touch the patty at the start of cooking: if you try to move it too soon, it will stick, and you won't be able to turn it.

Finally, once the meat is seared underneath, turn the patty over and press down on it with your spatula for about 10 seconds, so that the heat can diffuse through the meat more rapidly, which will help form a 'crust' on the other side. Only turn the patty once.

STEP 2: FOR LONGER COOKING, TURN THE HEAT DOWN

Once the meat is seared on both sides, reduce the heat to continue cooking through to the middle, without burning the crust, and so the meat does not dry out.

If you only want to sear the meat on one side, reduce the heat before turning it over.

5 DEGREES OF DONENESS

Blue: 1 minute on each side.

Bloody: 2 minutes on each side (this is the preferred method for the recipes in this book).

Rare: 3 minutes on each side.

Medium: 4 minutes on each side.

Well done: 5 minutes on each side.

Never eat veal or lamb 'blue' or 'bloody'; they should always be cooked to at least rare or medium.

Fancy
FLOURISHES

SAY CHEESE!

The best cheeses for burgers are those that melt well, or at least are moist enough to soften.

Classic contenders include cheddar, Swiss, gouda, American sliced cheese and monterey jack, but also don't be afraid to try softer cheeses like gorgonzola, brie, raclette, goat's cheese, stilton, blue cheese and gruyère, if you'd like to fancy things up.

For the perfect cheese consistency, we melt the cheese separately in a small non-stick saucepan over low heat before using it on our burgers – the cheese must be melted and hot, but not browned.

HERBAL FLAIR

Fresh herbs such as parsley, coriander (cilantro), mint, chives and tarragon can enhance the taste of burgers. Chop the herbs by hand at the last moment, and add them to the burger just before serving, so their flavour is as fresh as possible.

GIVE YOUR VEGIES A GRILLING

We recommend grilling vegetables such as eggplant (aubergine), zucchini (courgette) and capsicum (bell pepper) before using them on a burger.

Choose seasonal vegetables, and marinate them beforehand if you wish (in a mix of olive oil and fresh

herbs, for example), to give them as much flavour as possible.

Cook them on the grill, or in a frying pan, and stop cooking while they are still a bit crunchy.

Onions and tomatoes are other good candidates for grilling, adding a sweet, candied and uplifting note to your burgers.

Be sure to add your grilled vegies to the burgers warm, so the hamburgers keep all their heat.

Take care with 'wet' vegetables such as fresh tomato, which can leak juice that can soak the bun – detrimental to a good burger!

Spiced barbecue
SAUCE

4 tablespoons barbecue sauce

1 teaspoon ground cumin

1 teaspoon paprika

juice of ½ lemon

Simply combine all the ingredients!

Onion cocktail
SAUCE

1 egg yolk

1 tablespoon mustard

100 ml (3½ fl oz) sunflower oil

2 tablespoons ketchup

½ red onion, finely chopped

Mix together the egg yolk and mustard. Whisking vigorously, slowly add the oil, until emulsified. Stir the ketchup and onion through until well combined.

EACH SAUCE MAKES ENOUGH FOR 4 BURGERS

Maple mustard
SAUCE

1 egg yolk

1 tablespoon mustard

100 ml (3½ fl oz) sunflower oil

1 teaspoon maple syrup

a dash of Tabasco

a few drops of sherry vinegar

Mix together the egg yolk and mustard. Whisking vigorously, slowly add the oil, until emulsified. Whisk in the maple syrup, Tabasco and vinegar until well combined.

Creamy cheese + chive
SAUCE

100 g (3½ oz) mascarpone

1 teaspoon mustard

a pinch of sweet paprika

5–6 chives, finely chopped

Mix together the mascarpone, mustard and paprika. Stir the chives through.

HOT TIP!

For olive-studded buns,
add 125 g (4½ oz/1 cup)
pitted black olives to the dough
before the first rising.

For raisin-nut buns, add 60 g
(2 oz/½ cup) chopped walnuts
and 60 g (2 oz/½ cup) raisins
to the dough before the
first rising.

The best HAMBURGER BUNS!

600 g (1 lb 5 oz/4 cups) plain (all-purpose) flour, plus extra for dusting

25 g (1 oz) fresh yeast, finely crumbled

1 tablespoon sugar

1 teaspoon salt

180 ml (6 fl oz) lukewarm skim milk

150 ml (5 fl oz) lukewarm water

1 egg

30 g (1 oz) butter, melted

sesame seeds, for sprinkling

In a bowl, mix together the flour, yeast, sugar and salt. Make a well in the centre, then add the milk, water, egg and butter. Mix until the dough comes together into a ball that no longer sticks to the side of the bowl.

Turn the dough out onto a floured work surface and knead until soft, elastic and smooth. Shape into a ball, then place in a clean oiled bowl. Cover with a damp cloth and leave to rise in a warm place for 1½ hours.

Divide the dough into 12 equal portions. On a floured surface, roll each piece of dough into a small ball. Cover with a cloth and rest for 10 minutes.

Flatten the dough balls into bun shapes. Working one at a time, lightly brush the top and side of a bun with water, then sprinkle with sesame seeds, lightly pressing them on so they adhere. Repeat with the remaining buns and place on a baking tray lined with baking paper. Cover with a cloth and leave to rise for a further 1 hour.

Preheat the oven to 200°C (400°F) and put a small container of water inside the oven for humidity while baking.

Bake the buns for 15–20 minutes, or until golden. Leave to cool on a wire rack. Any buns that aren't needed within a day or two can be frozen for later use.

French
FRIES

800 g (1 lb 12 oz) good 'chipping' potatoes, such as bintje, yukon gold, king edward, desiree, maris piper or sebago

sunflower or peanut oil, for deep-frying

salt, for sprinkling

garlic powder, for sprinkling

paprika, for sprinkling

Peel the potatoes and wash them. Cut into 1 cm (½ in) thick slices, then cut them into chips. Soak in warm water for 5 minutes, stir well, then drain. Wipe the chips with a clean tea towel to remove the starch.

In a deep-fryer, heat the oil to 160°C (320°F). Carefully add the chips and cook for 6–7 minutes, until they are beginning to soften inside.

Scoop the chips out of the oil, drain well, then let them sit for at least 20 minutes.

Reheat the oil, then plunge the chips back into the oil and let them brown for 1–2 minutes.

Scoop the chips out and drain on paper towel to remove as much oil as possible. Sprinkle generously with salt, and garlic powder and paprika to taste.

HOT TIP #1

If you don't have a deep-fryer, you can use a large heavy-based saucepan. Add the chips to the oil when it starts to simmer.

HOT TIP #2

Add a garlic clove to the frying oil for added flavour.

HOT TIP #3

For fancy fries, cook them in hot duck fat instead of vegetable oil.

Coleslaw

300 g (10½ oz) white cabbage

1 large carrot

1 cooked beetroot (beet)

ORANGE MUSTARD MAYO

3 tablespoons mustard

4 egg yolks

100 ml (3½ fl oz) sunflower oil

1 teaspoon ricotta or softened cream cheese

1 tablespoon orange juice

50 ml (1¾ fl oz) Tabasco or other hot chilli sauce

1 teaspoon sherry vinegar

a few coriander (cilantro) or flat-leaf (Italian) parsley leaves, chopped

Grate the cabbage and carrot. Peel the beetroot and cut it into small cubes. Place all the vegetables in a bowl.

To make the orange mustard mayo, mix together the mustard and egg yolks. Add the oil in a slow stream, whisking to combine. When the sauce has emulsified, stir in the remaining ingredients and season with salt and pepper.

Toss the mayo through the vegetable mixture and serve.

BEEF BURGERS WITH BRIE

600 g (1 lb 5 oz) minced (ground) beef

a splash of sunflower or vegetable oil

200 g (7 oz) brie or camembert, roughly chopped

4 hamburger buns (page 85)

1 red onion, sliced into rings

handful of salad leaves

COCKTAIL SAUCE

1 egg yolk

1 tablespoon mustard

100 ml (3½ fl oz) sunflower oil

2 tablespoons ketchup

To make the cocktail sauce, mix together the egg yolk and mustard. Add the oil in a slow stream, whisking to combine. When the sauce has emulsified, stir in the ketchup and season well with salt and pepper.

Preheat the grill (broiler) to high.

To make the burger patties, season the meat with salt and pepper, divide into four equal-sized balls and form into patties. Heat a little oil in a frying pan over high heat and cook the patties for 3–4 minutes on each side (for medium–rare), making sure they don't burn.

While the patties are cooking, slice the buns open and place them, cut side up, under the grill for 1 minute, until warmed through and golden.

Meanwhile, warm the cheese in a small saucepan over low heat for 1–2 minutes, until melted.

To assemble, spread the cocktail sauce on the cut sides of the buns. Place the patties on the bottom buns, then top with the melted cheese, onion rings and salad leaves. Put the bun lids on top and serve immediately.

HOT TIP!

For a tangier sauce, add a drop of worcestershire sauce, a few drops of Tabasco or other hot chilli sauce, and some finely chopped pickles.

HOT TIP!

When cooking the bacon, you can add a splash of balsamic vinegar for a touch of caramelised sweetness.

Bacon + cheddar
BURGERS

600 g (1 lb 5 oz) minced (ground) beef

a splash of sunflower or vegetable oil

120 g (4½ oz) streaky bacon rashers (slices)

4 hamburger buns (page 85)

200 g (7 oz) cheddar

Cocktail sauce (see page 90)

1 red onion, sliced into rings

Preheat the grill (broiler) to high.

To make the burger patties, season the meat with salt and pepper, divide into four equal-sized balls and form into patties. Heat a little oil in a frying pan over high heat and cook the patties for 3–4 minutes on each side (for medium–rare), making sure they don't burn.

In a separate frying pan, fry the bacon over high heat for 1 minute on each side, until nice and crisp but not burned.

While the patties are cooking, slice the buns open and place them, cut side up, under the grill for 1 minute, until warmed through and golden.

Meanwhile, warm the cheese in a small saucepan over low heat for 1–2 minutes, until melted.

To assemble, spread the cocktail sauce on the cut sides of the buns. Place the patties on the bottom buns, then top with the melted cheese, bacon and onion rings. Put the bun lids on top and serve immediately.

French CHEESEBURGERS

600 g (1 lb 5 oz) minced (ground) beef

a splash of sunflower or vegetable oil

4 hamburger buns (page 85)

200 g (7 oz) raclette, or a mild semi-firm white rind cheese such as tomme de Savoie, or a French blue-veined cheese such as fourme d'Ambert, roughly chopped

Cocktail sauce (see page 90)

1 red onion, sliced into rings

1 tablespoon finely chopped chives or parsley

Preheat the grill (broiler) to high.

To make the burger patties, season the meat with salt and pepper, divide into four equal-sized balls and form into patties. Heat a little oil in a frying pan over high heat and cook the patties for 3–4 minutes on each side (for medium–rare), making sure they don't burn.

While the patties are cooking, slice the buns open and place them, cut side up, under the grill for 1 minute, until warmed through and golden.

Meanwhile, warm the cheese in a small saucepan over low heat for 1–2 minutes, until melted.

To assemble, spread the cocktail sauce on the cut sides of the buns. Place the patties on the bottom buns, then top with the melted cheese and onion rings, before sprinkling with the herbs. Put the bun lids on top and serve immediately.

HOT TIP!

Instead of raclette you could use a good melting cheese such as Swiss cheese, jarlsberg, emmental, or a mild gruyère.

For a sweet contrast with the saltiness of the cheese, sauté the onion with a splash of balsamic vinegar for a few minutes.

HOT TIP!

For extra flavour, use a
sharp, tangy blue cheese
such as Roquefort.

Beef + blue cheese
BURGERS

4 hamburger buns (page 85)

600 g (1 lb 5 oz) minced (ground) beef

2 tablespoons finely diced pickled onion

a splash of sunflower or vegetable oil

200 g (7 oz) blue cheese, roughly chopped

1 red onion, sliced into rings

a handful of baby spinach leaves

SWEET SPICED MUSTARD SAUCE

1 egg yolk

1 tablespoon hot mustard

1 teaspoon spiced mustard (such as Savora)

100 ml (3½ fl oz) sunflower oil

1 teaspoon maple syrup

a few coriander (cilantro) leaves, finely chopped

To make the mustard sauce, mix together the egg yolk and both the mustards. Add the oil in a slow stream, whisking to combine. When the sauce has emulsified, stir in the maple syrup and coriander.

Preheat the grill (broiler) to high.

To make the burger patties, combine the meat and the pickled onion and season with salt and pepper. Divide into four equal-sized balls and form into patties. Heat a little oil in a frying pan over high heat and cook the patties for 3–4 minutes on each side (for medium–rare), making sure they don't burn.

While the patties are cooking, slice the buns open and place them, cut side up, under the grill for 1 minute, until warmed through and golden.

Meanwhile, warm the cheese in a small saucepan over low heat for 1–2 minutes, until melted.

To assemble, spread the mustard sauce on the cut sides of the buns. Place the patties on the bottom buns, then top with the melted cheese, onion rings and spinach leaves. Put the bun lids on top and serve immediately.

Paprika chicken burgers
WITH TARRAGON MAYO

2 tablespoons paprika

2 tablespoons garlic powder

4 x 120 g (4½ oz) boneless,
skinless chicken breasts

a splash of sunflower or vegetable oil

4 hamburger buns (page 85)

200 g (7 oz) brie or camembert,
roughly chopped

1 onion, sliced into rings

TARRAGON MAYO

1 egg yolk

1 tablespoon mustard

100 ml (3½ fl oz) sunflower oil

1 teaspoon soy sauce

a few fresh tarragon leaves,
finely chopped

To make the tarragon mayo, mix together the egg yolk and mustard. Add the oil in a slow stream, whisking to combine. When the sauce has emulsified, stir in the soy sauce and tarragon.

Preheat the grill (broiler) to high.

Mix together the paprika and garlic powder. Brush the chicken fillets on both sides with a little oil, then coat with the spice mix. Heat a little oil in a frying pan over medium heat and cook the chicken for 4–6 minutes on each side. Season with salt and pepper.

While the chicken fillets are cooking, slice the buns open and place them, cut side up, under the grill for 1 minute, until warmed through and golden.

Meanwhile, warm the cheese in a small saucepan over low heat for 1–2 minutes, until melted.

To assemble, spread the tarragon mayo on the cut sides of the buns. Place the chicken fillets on the bottom buns, then top with the melted cheese and onion rings. Put the bun lids on top and serve immediately.

HOT TIP!

If you can get it, Saint-Nectaire is wonderful on this burger. It is a semi-soft French cheese with a sweet, creamy, nutty flavour.

HOT TIP!

If your patty mixture doesn't hold together very well, add a beaten egg yolk and some breadcrumbs.

VEAL BURGERS
with eggplant + blue cheese

a splash of sunflower
or vegetable oil

250 g (9 oz) eggplant
(aubergine), sliced

600 g (1 lb 5 oz) minced
(ground) veal

200 g (7 oz) blue cheese,
roughly chopped

a small handful of coriander
(cilantro) leaves

4 walnuts, crushed

CARAMEL MUSTARD SAUCE

1 egg yolk

1 tablespoon mustard

100 ml (3½ fl oz) sunflower oil

1 teaspoon caramel syrup

a dash of Tabasco or
other hot chilli sauce

a dash of sherry vinegar

To make the mustard sauce, mix together the egg yolk and mustard. Add the oil in a slow stream, whisking to combine. When the sauce has emulsified, stir in the caramel syrup, Tabasco and sherry vinegar.

Heat a little oil in a frying pan over medium heat and cook the eggplant for a few minutes on each side. Keep warm until ready to serve.

Preheat the grill (broiler) to high.

To make the burger patties, season the meat with salt and pepper, divide into four equal-sized balls and form into patties. Heat a little oil in a frying pan over high heat and cook for 3–4 minutes on each side (for medium–rare), making sure they don't burn.

While the patties are cooking, slice the buns open and place them, cut side up, under the grill for 1 minute, until warmed through and golden.

Meanwhile, warm the cheese in a small saucepan over low heat for 1–2 minutes, until melted.

To assemble, spread the mustard sauce on the cut sides of the buns. Place the patties on the bottom buns, then top with the melted cheese, eggplant, coriander and crushed walnuts. Put the bun lids on top and serve immediately.

LAMB BURGERS
with zucchini + goat's cheese

100 ml (3½ fl oz) olive oil

juice of 1 lemon

250 g (9 oz) zucchini (courgette), sliced

600 g (1 lb 5 oz) minced (ground) lamb

a splash of sunflower or vegetable oil

4 hamburger buns (page 85)

200 g (7 oz) goat's cheese

a small handful of mint leaves

HOT MUSTARD SAUCE

1 egg yolk

1 tablespoon hot mustard

1 teaspoon yellow American mustard

100 ml (3½ fl oz) sunflower oil

a dash of Tabasco or other hot chilli sauce

Combine the olive oil and lemon juice in a small bowl. Add the zucchini and leave to marinate for 1 hour.

To make the mustard sauce, mix together the egg yolk and mustards. Add the oil in a slow stream, whisking to combine. When the sauce has emulsified, stir in the Tabasco.

Heat a frying pan over medium heat and cook the zucchini for 4–5 minutes, turning occasionally. Keep warm until ready to serve.

Preheat the grill (broiler) to high.

To make the burger patties, season the meat with salt and pepper, divide into four equal-sized balls and form into patties. Heat a little oil in a frying pan over high heat and cook for 4–5 minutes on each side (for medium), making sure they don't burn.

While the patties are cooking, slice the buns open and place them, cut side up, under the grill for 1 minute, until warmed through and golden.

Meanwhile, warm the cheese in a small saucepan over low heat for 1–2 minutes, until melted.

To assemble, spread the mustard sauce on the cut sides of the buns. Place the patties on the bottom buns, then top with the melted cheese, zucchini and mint. Put the bun lids on top and serve immediately.

HOT TIP!

For an extra punch of flavour, grate a little garlic into the burger mixture.

(THREE-MEAT) BURGERS WITH CAPSICUM

MAKES 4

2 tablespoons olive oil

juice of 1 lemon

1 garlic clove, crushed

1 red capsicum (bell pepper), cut into strips

200 g (7 oz) minced (ground) veal

200 g (7 oz) minced (ground) lamb

200 g (7 oz) minced (ground) beef

70 g (2½ oz/¼ cup) tomato paste (concentrated purée)

a splash of sunflower or vegetable oil

4 hamburger buns (page 85)

200 g (7 oz) Swiss cheese, raclette or monterey jack, roughly chopped

a few chervil leaves, finely chopped

ONION COCKTAIL SAUCE

1 egg yolk

1 tablespoon mustard

100 ml (3½ fl oz) sunflower oil

2 tablespoons ketchup

½ red onion, finely chopped

Combine the olive oil, lemon juice and garlic in a dish. Add the capsicum and leave to marinate for 15 minutes.

To make the cocktail sauce, mix together the egg yolk and mustard. Add the oil in a slow stream, whisking to combine. When the sauce has emulsified, stir in the ketchup and onion.

Heat a frying pan over medium heat and cook the capsicum for 10 minutes, turning occasionally. Keep warm until ready to serve.

Preheat the grill (broiler) to high.

To make the burger patties, combine the meat and tomato paste and season with salt and pepper. Divide into four equal-sized balls and form into patties.

Heat a little oil in a frying pan over high heat and cook the patties for 4–5 minutes on each side (for medium), making sure they don't burn.

While the patties are cooking, slice the buns open and place them, cut side up, under the grill for 1 minute, until warmed through and golden.

Meanwhile, warm the cheese in a small saucepan over low heat for 1–2 minutes, until melted.

To assemble, spread the cocktail sauce on the cut sides of the buns. Place the patties on the bottom buns, then top with the melted cheese, capsicum and chervil. Put the bun lids on top and serve immediately.

BLACK PUDDING BURGERS
with apple + bacon

600 g (1 lb 5 oz) black pudding sausages

a splash of sunflower or vegetable oil

1 apple, peeled and diced

1 onion, diced

4 large bacon rashers (slices)

4 hamburger buns (page 85)

Remove the meat from the sausages and place in a bowl.

Heat a little oil in a frying pan over medium heat and sauté the apple and onion for 5–10 minutes, until soft and caramelised. Set aside to cool for a few minutes, then combine with the sausage meat. Divide into four equal-sized balls and form into patties.

Preheat the grill (broiler) to high.

Heat a little more oil in a frying pan over high heat and cook the patties for 3–4 minutes on each side (for medium–rare), making sure they don't burn.

Meanwhile, cook the bacon in another frying pan.

While the patties are cooking, slice the buns open and place them, cut side up, under the grill for 1 minute, until warmed through and golden.

To assemble, place the patties on the bottom buns, then top with the bacon. Put the bun lids on top and serve immediately.

HOT TIP!

Spread the buns with
a thin layer of your
favourite mustard.

HOT TIP!

To keep the salmon moist and juicy, you could cook it under the grill (broiler) instead of frying it.

(SALMON) BURGERS WITH HOLLANDAISE

1 tablespoon butter

1 tablespoon sunflower oil

4 x 200 g (7 oz) salmon fillets, pin bones removed

2 lemons, 1 thinly sliced

8 semi-dried (sun-blushed) tomatoes

1 tablespoon balsamic vinegar

4 hamburger buns (page 85)

coarse salt, for sprinkling

HOLLANDAISE SAUCE

3 egg yolks

juice of 1 lemon

300 ml (10½ fl oz) melted butter

To make the hollandaise sauce, put the egg yolks in a saucepan with the lemon juice and a splash of water. Mix with a whisk, then place over medium heat and stir continuously as the mixture warms through. A little bit at a time, stir in the melted butter, mixing well to obtain a smooth sauce. Set aside and keep warm.

Preheat the grill (broiler) to high.

Warm the butter and oil in a frying pan and cook the salmon fillets over medium heat for 3–4 minutes on each side, until just done. Squeeze the juice of the whole lemon onto the fish.

Meanwhile, in a small frying pan, splash the tomatoes with the vinegar and warm over medium heat for 1–2 minutes.

While the salmon fillets are cooking, slice the buns open and place them, cut side up, under the grill for 1 minute, until warmed through and golden.

To assemble, place the salmon fillets on the bottom buns, sprinkle with salt, then top with the hollandaise sauce, lemon slices and tomatoes. Put the bun lids on top and serve immediately.

100 ml (3½ fl oz) olive oil
juice of 1 lemon
1 garlic clove, finely chopped
1 zucchini (courgette), sliced
1 yellow or red capsicum
(bell pepper), cut into strips
a splash of sunflower or vegetable oil
4 hamburger buns (page 85)
200 g (7 oz) brie or camembert,
roughly chopped

VEGIE BURGERS

2 tablespoons quinoa
425 g (15 oz) tin black beans,
rinsed and drained
½ capsicum (bell pepper),
finely diced
¼ red onion, finely diced
4 garlic cloves, chopped
45 g (1½ oz/½ cup) fresh
breadcrumbs
1 egg, lightly beaten
¼ teaspoon ground cumin
a pinch of salt
a few drops of Tabasco or
other hot chilli sauce

CREAMY CHEESE &
CHIVE SAUCE

100 g (3½ oz) mascarpone
1 teaspoon mustard
a pinch of sweet paprika
5–6 chives, finely chopped

BLACK BEAN + QUINOA
vegie burgers

MAKES 4

To make the burger patties, cook the quinoa in 100 ml (3½ fl oz) boiling water for 15–20 minutes. Put the beans in a bowl and mash with a fork. Add the quinoa and remaining burger ingredients and mix together well. Divide into four equal-sized balls and form into patties.

Meanwhile, combine the olive oil, lemon juice and garlic in a dish. Add the zucchini and capsicum and leave to marinate for 15 minutes.

To make the cheese and chive sauce, mix together the mascarpone, mustard and paprika. Stir the chives through.

Preheat the grill (broiler) to medium. Cook the zucchini and capsicum under the grill for 10 minutes. Keep warm.

Heat a little oil in a frying pan over medium heat and cook the

vegie patties for 4 minutes on each side, or until warmed through, making sure they don't burn.

While the patties are cooking, turn the grill (broiler) temperature up high. Slice the buns open and place them, cut side up, under the grill for 1 minute, until warmed through and golden.

Meanwhile, warm the brie or camembert in a small saucepan over low heat for 1–2 minutes, until melted.

To assemble, spread the cheese and chive sauce on the cut sides of the buns. Place the patties on the bottom buns, then top with the melted brie or camembert, zucchini and capsicum. Put the bun lids on top and serve immediately.

HOT TIP!

Add some caramelised
onion when assembling
the burgers.

Beef + herbed egg BURGERS

600 g (1 lb 5 oz) minced (ground) beef

a splash of sunflower or vegetable oil

4 free-range eggs

a few sprigs of mixed fresh herbs such as parsley, chives, chervil and tarragon, finely chopped

1 teaspoon paprika

4 hamburger buns (page 85)

200 g (7 oz) Swiss cheese, raclette or monterey jack, roughly chopped

Cocktail sauce (see page 90)

1 red onion, sliced into rings

a handful of salad leaves

Preheat the grill (broiler) to high.

To make the burger patties, season the meat with salt and pepper, divide into four equal-sized balls and form into patties. Heat some oil in a frying pan over high heat and cook the patties for 3–4 minutes on each side (for medium–rare), making sure they don't burn.

In another frying pan, heat another splash of oil. Crack the eggs into the pan and sprinkle the herbs on the whites. Cook the eggs for a few minutes, without turning.

When the whites are cooked, sprinkle the yolks with salt and the paprika. Be sure not to overcook the eggs – you want the yolks to remain soft and runny.

While the patties and eggs are cooking, slice the buns open and place them, cut side up, under the grill for 1 minute, until warmed through and golden.

Meanwhile, warm the cheese in a small saucepan over low heat for 1–2 minutes, until melted.

To assemble, spread the cocktail sauce on the cut sides of the buns. Place the patties on the bottom buns, then top with the melted cheese, onion, salad leaves and eggs. Put the bun lids on top and serve immediately.

Tuna tartare BURGERS

800 g (1 lb 12 oz) raw tuna

4 hamburger buns (page 85)

a handful of salad leaves

TARTARE SAUCE

2 egg yolks

1 teaspoon mustard

1 tablespoon olive oil

juice of 1 lemon

3 French shallots, finely chopped

1 tablespoon chopped chives

2 cornichons, finely diced

To make the tartare sauce, mix together the egg yolks and mustard. Whisk in the oil and lemon juice, then stir the remaining ingredients through.

To make the tuna patties, chop the tuna with a knife, as fine or as coarsely as you like, then mix it with your tartare sauce and season with salt and pepper. Divide into four equal-sized balls and shape each into a steak shape. Cover with plastic wrap and refrigerate for 2 hours.

When you're ready to eat, preheat the grill (broiler) to high.

Slice the buns open and place them, cut side up, under the grill for 1 minute, until warmed through and golden.

To assemble, place the patties onto the bottom buns and top with salad leaves. Put the bun lids on top and serve immediately.

HOT TIP!

You can briefly warm the tuna patties under the grill before assembling the burgers.

Jumbo double-cheese
BURGERS

400 g (14 oz) minced (ground) beef

400 g (14 oz) minced (ground) veal

a splash of sunflower or vegetable oil

4 hamburger buns (page 85)

200 g (7 oz) blue cheese, chopped

200 g (7 oz) Swiss cheese, raclette or monterey jack, roughly chopped

12 semi-dried (sun-blushed) tomatoes

a handful of salad leaves

1 teaspoon chopped flat-leaf (Italian) parsley

TANGY COCKTAIL SAUCE

1 egg yolk

1 tablespoon mustard

100 ml (3½ fl oz) sunflower oil

2 tablespoons tomato ketchup

½ red onion, finely chopped

a few drops of Tabasco or other hot chilli sauce

a dash of sherry vinegar

a dash of worcestershire sauce

To make the cocktail sauce, mix together the egg yolk and mustard. Add the oil in a slow stream, whisking to combine. When the sauce has emulsified, stir in the remaining ingredients.

Preheat the grill (broiler) to high.

To make the burger patties, season the beef with salt and pepper, divide into four equal-sized balls and form into patties. Do the same with the veal.

Heat a little oil in a frying pan over high heat. Cook the veal patties for 5 minutes on each side, making sure they don't burn; the beef patties will only need 3 minutes on each side. Keep warm.

While the patties are cooking, slice the buns open and place them, cut side up, under the grill for 1 minute, until warmed through and golden.

Meanwhile, warm the cheeses separately in two small saucepans over low heat for 1–2 minutes, until melted.

To assemble, spread the cocktail sauce on the cut sides of the buns. Place the veal patties on the bottom buns, then top with the melted blue cheese and half the tomatoes. Add all the salad leaves. Place the beef patties on top, then the melted Swiss cheese and remaining tomatoes. Sprinkle with the parsley, put the bun lids on top and serve immediately.

BEEF & RÖSTI
burgers

600 g (1 lb 5 oz) minced (ground) beef
a pinch of ground cumin
1 tablespoon white wine
a splash of sunflower or vegetable oil
4 hamburger buns (page 85)
200 g (7 oz) sharp cheddar or monterey jack, roughly chopped

POTATO RÖSTI

2 bintje potatoes, or other good frying potatoes, peeled
1 small red onion, peeled
1 tablespoon plain (all-purpose) flour
1 egg, lightly beaten
a splash of sunflower or vegetable oil

CHERVIL MAYO

1 egg yolk
1 tablespoon mustard
100 ml (3½ fl oz) sunflower oil
a pinch of chopped fresh chervil

To make the chervil mayo, mix together the egg yolk and mustard. Add the oil in a slow stream, whisking to combine. When the sauce has emulsified, stir in the chervil and season with salt and pepper.

To make the rösti, grate the potatoes and onion into a bowl. Add the flour and egg and season with salt and pepper. Mix together, then divide into four equal portions. Heat a little oil in a frying pan over medium heat and add the potato mounds, spacing them well apart. Flatten them into patties and brown them on both sides. Keep warm.

To make the burger patties, combine the meat, cumin and wine and season with salt and pepper. Divide into four equal-sized balls and form into patties.

Heat a little oil in a separate frying pan over high heat and cook the patties for 3–4 minutes on each side (for medium–rare), making sure they don't burn.

Preheat the grill (broiler) to high.

While the patties are cooking, slice the buns open and place them, cut side up, under the grill for 1 minute, until warmed through and golden.

Meanwhile, warm the cheese in a small saucepan over low heat for 1–2 minutes, until melted.

To assemble, spread the chervil mayo on the cut sides of the buns. Place the patties on the bottom buns, then top with the melted cheese and a rösti. Put the bun lids on top and serve immediately.

HOT TIP!

Add some chopped
fried bacon to your
rösti mixture before
cooking them.

HOT TIP!

You could add a splash of beer to the cocktail sauce.

BEEF BURGERS
with braised witlof

600 g (1 lb 5 oz) minced (ground) beef

a splash of sunflower or vegetable oil

4 hamburger buns (page 85)

200 g (7 oz) brie or camembert, roughly chopped

1 tablespoon finely chopped flat-leaf (Italian) parsley

BRAISED WITLOF

2 tablespoons butter

1 witlof (chicory), leaves separated

1 teaspoon sugar

BALSAMIC COCKTAIL SAUCE

1 egg yolk

1 tablespoon mustard

100 ml (3½ fl oz) sunflower oil

2 tablespoons tomato ketchup

a few dashes of balsamic vinegar

To make the cocktail sauce, mix together the egg yolk and mustard. Add the oil in a slow stream, whisking to combine. When the sauce has emulsified, stir in the ketchup and vinegar and season with salt and pepper.

To make the burger patties, season the meat with salt and pepper, divide into four equal-sized balls and form into patties. Heat a little oil in a frying pan over high heat and cook for 4 minutes on each side, making sure they don't burn.

Meanwhile, to braise the witlof, melt the butter in a separate frying pan over medium heat. Add the witlof leaves, sprinkle with the sugar and cook for about 4 minutes, until tender and caramelised.

Preheat the grill (broiler) to high.

While the patties are cooking, slice the buns open and place them, cut side up, under the grill for 1 minute, until warmed through and golden.

Meanwhile, warm the cheese in a small saucepan over low heat for 1–2 minutes, until melted.

To assemble, spread the cocktail sauce on the cut sides of the buns. Place the patties on the bottom buns, then top with the melted cheese, braised witlof and parsley. Put the bun lids on top and serve immediately.

Beef + smoked bacon burgers
WITH RACLETTE

1 tablespoon butter

1 large onion, finely chopped

600 g (1 lb 5 oz) minced (ground) beef

a splash of sunflower or vegetable oil

4 slices thick-cut smoked bacon

4 hamburger buns (page 85)

200 g (7 oz) raclette, Swiss cheese or monterey jack, roughly chopped

WHITE WINE SAUCE

100 g (3½ oz) crème fraîche

1 teaspoon mustard

50 ml (1¾ fl oz) white wine

Melt the butter in a frying pan over medium heat. Add the onion and cook for about 1 minute, until starting to soften. Turn down the heat and cook for another 7 minutes, or until soft and caramelised. Leave to cool.

To make the white wine sauce, mix the crème fraîche with the mustard and the wine. Warm it up in a small saucepan and season with salt and pepper. Keep warm.

Preheat the grill (broiler) to high.

To make the burger patties, combine the meat with the caramelised onion and season with salt and pepper. Divide into four equal-sized balls and form into patties. Heat a little oil in a frying pan over high heat and cook for 4 minutes on each side, making sure they don't burn.

Meawnhile, cook the bacon in a separate pan.

While the bacon and patties are cooking, slice the buns open and place them, cut side up, under the grill for 1 minute, until warmed through and golden.

Meanwhile, warm the cheese in a small saucepan over low heat for 1–2 minutes, until melted.

To assemble, spread the white wine sauce on the cut sides of the buns. Place the patties on the bottom buns, then top with the melted cheese and bacon. Put the bun lids on top and serve immediately.

HOT TIP!

When assembling
the burgers, sprinkle
the melted cheese with
freshly grated nutmeg.

HOT TIP!

If you like, you can heat the foie gras for 45 seconds on each side in a frying pan before assembling the burgers.

DUCK BURGERS
with foie gras + pear

2 pears, peeled and sliced into thin wedges

4 hamburger buns (page 85)

4 teaspoons plum jam

400 g (14 oz) foie gras, sliced into 8 portions

150 g (5½ oz) cured duck breast, sliced

Preheat the grill (broiler) to high.

Cook the pear slices in a frying pan over medium heat until golden brown, turning to cook both sides.

While the pears are cooking, slice the buns open and place them, cut side up, under the grill for 1 minute, until warmed through and golden.

To assemble, spread the jam on the cut sides of the buns. Place half the foie gras slices on the bottom buns, then top with half the duck slices. Repeat with the remaining foie gras and duck, then top with the pears. Put the bun lids on top and serve immediately.

BEEF BURGERS
with black radish

600 g (1 lb 5 oz) minced (ground) beef

a splash of sunflower or vegetable oil

4 hamburger buns (page 85)

200 g (7 oz) sharp cheddar

12 thin slices of black radish

Tangy cocktail sauce (see page 117)

1 tablespoon chopped flat-leaf (Italian) parsley

Preheat the grill (broiler) to high.

To make the burger patties, season the meat with salt and pepper, divide into four equal-sized balls and form into patties. Heat a little oil in a frying pan over high heat and cook for 4 minutes on each side, making sure they don't burn.

While the patties are cooking, slice the buns open and place them, cut side up, under the grill for 1 minute, until warmed through and golden.

Meanwhile, warm the cheese in a small saucepan over low heat for 1–2 minutes, until melted.

To assemble, place the patties on the bottom buns, then top with the melted cheese, then the cocktail sauce. Sprinkle with the parsley, then add the radish. Put the bun lids on top and serve immediately.

HOT TIP!

If unavailable, you can replace the black radish with regular radish.

HOT TIP!

When making the
parmesan crisps, add a
pinch of garlic powder
to the grated cheese.

VEAL BURGERS
with parmesan crisps

2 tablespoons grated parmesan

600 g (1 lb 5 oz) minced (ground) veal

a splash of sunflower or vegetable oil

4 hamburger buns (page 85)

Maple mustard sauce (page 83)

4 semi-dried (sun-blushed) tomatoes

a small handful of basil leaves

Preheat the grill (broiler) to high. Line a baking tray with baking paper.

To make the parmesan crisps, place four small piles of the grated parmesan on the lined baking tray, well spaced from each other. Spread them into discs and cook under the grill for 2–3 minutes. Remove and keep warm.

To make the burger patties, season the meat with salt and pepper, divide into four equal-sized balls and form into patties. Heat a little oil in a frying pan over high heat and cook for 4 minutes on each side, making sure they don't burn.

While the patties are cooking, slice the buns open and place them, cut side up, under the grill for 1 minute, until warmed through and golden.

To assemble, spread the maple mustard sauce on the cut sides of the buns. Place the patties on the bottom buns, then top with the tomatoes, basil leaves and parmesan crisps. Put the bun lids on top and serve immediately.

Crumbed chicken burgers
WITH CAMEMBERT

MAKES 4

2 tablespoons paprika

2 tablespoons garlic powder

4 x 120 g (4½ oz) boneless,
skinless chicken breasts, flattened

1 egg

4 tablespoons breadcrumbs

a splash of sunflower or vegetable oil

4 hamburger buns (page 85)

200 g (7 oz) camembert, chopped

Maple mustard sauce (page 83)

8 semi-dried (sun-blushed) tomatoes

1 teaspoon finely chopped tarragon

In a shallow bowl, mix together the paprika, garlic powder and some salt and pepper. Lightly beat the egg in a small bowl. Put the breadcrumbs on a plate. Dredge the chicken fillets on both sides in the beaten egg, then the paprika mixture, and finally in the breadcrumbs.

Heat a little oil in a frying pan over medium heat. Cook the crumbed chicken for about 5 minutes on each side, making sure the crumbs don't burn.

Meanwhile, preheat the grill (broiler) to high. Slice the buns open and place them, cut side up, under the grill for 1 minute, until warmed through and golden.

Warm the cheese in a small saucepan over low heat for 1–2 minutes, until melted.

To assemble, spread the maple mustard sauce on the cut sides of the buns. Place the chicken on the bottom buns, then top with the melted cheese, tomatoes and a pinch of tarragon. Put the bun lids on top and serve immediately.

Beer-braised steak burgers
WITH COLESLAW

a splash of sunflower or
vegetable oil

600 g (1 lb 5 oz) chuck steak, diced

1 carrot, finely diced

½ onion, finely diced

1 garlic clove, finely chopped

3 tablespoons tomato paste
(concentrated purée)

500 ml (17 fl oz/2 cups) beer

4 hamburger buns (page 85)

Spiced barbecue sauce (page 83)

Coleslaw (page 89)

To make the burger patties, heat a little oil in a flameproof casserole dish over medium heat and brown the diced steak on all sides. Add the carrot, onion and garlic and stir for a minute or two. Add the tomato paste and stir in the beer, mixing well to deglaze the pan of any cooked-on bits. Season with salt and pepper. Cover and cook over low heat for 1 hour, until the meat is tender. Allow to cool.

Divide the steak mixture into four equal portions, then form into patties. Heat a little oil in a frying pan over high heat and cook for 4 minutes on each side. Season again with salt and pepper.

While the meat is cooking, preheat the grill (broiler) to high. Slice the buns open and place them, cut side up, under the grill for 1 minute, until warmed through and golden.

To assemble, spread the barbecue sauce on the cut sides of the buns. Place the patties on the bottom buns, then top with coleslaw. Put the bun lids on top and serve immediately.

BEEF BURGERS
with fig chutney + blue cheese

MAKES 4

600 g (1 lb 5 oz) minced (ground) beef

a splash of sunflower or vegetable oil

4 hamburger buns (page 85)

200 g (7 oz) blue cheese

3–4 tablespoons yellow American mustard

4 tablespoons fig chutney

1 teaspoon finely chopped flat-leaf (Italian) parsley

Preheat the grill (broiler) to high.

To make the burger patties, season the meat with salt and pepper, divide into four equal-sized balls and form into patties. Heat a little oil in a frying pan over high heat and cook for 4–5 minutes on each side, making sure they don't burn.

While the patties are cooking, slice the buns open and place them, cut side up, under the grill for 1 minute, until warmed through and golden.

Meanwhile, warm the cheese in a small saucepan over low heat for 1–2 minutes, until melted.

To assemble, spread the mustard on the cut sides of the buns. Place the patties on the bottom buns, then top with the chutney, melted cheese and parsley. Put the bun lids on top and serve immediately.

HOT TIP!

Add a slice of cooked
bacon to each burger.

HOT TIP!

For extra spice, add a few good pinches of espalette pepper to the patty mixture.

Lamb + chorizo BURGERS

a splash of sunflower or vegetable oil

250 g (9 oz) chorizo sausage, cut into small cubes

600 g (1 lb 5 oz) minced (ground) lamb

4 hamburger buns (page 85)

200 g (7 oz) Swiss cheese, raclette or monterey jack, roughly chopped

Maple mustard sauce (page 83)

a handful of mesclun salad leaves

To make the burger patties, heat a little oil in a frying pan over medium–high heat and fry the chorizo for about 3 minutes. Set aside to cool for a few minutes, then combine with the lamb and season with salt and pepper.

Divide the meat mixture into four equal-sized balls and form into patties. Heat a little oil in a frying pan over high heat and cook for 4–5 minutes on each side, making sure they don't burn.

While the patties are cooking, preheat the grill (broiler) to high. Slice the buns open and place them, cut side up, under the grill for 1 minute, until warmed through and golden.

Meanwhile, warm the cheese in a small saucepan over low heat for 1–2 minutes, until melted.

To assemble, spread the maple mustard sauce on the cut sides of the buns. Place the patties on the bottom buns, then top with the melted cheese and salad leaves. Put the bun lids on top and serve immediately.

PORK BURGERS WITH MAPLE SYRUP

a splash of sunflower or vegetable oil

800 g (1 lb 12 oz) boneless pork loin pieces

4 tablespoons maple syrup

4 hamburger buns (page 85)

200 g (7 oz) cheddar, roughly chopped

Spiced barbecue sauce (page 83)

crispy fried shallots, for sprinkling

2 teaspoons chopped chives

Heat a little oil in a frying pan and brown the pork pieces in a frying pan for about 4 minutes on each side. Remove from the pan, season with salt and pepper, then slice the pork pieces into strips. Put them back in the frying pan, drizzle with the maple syrup and fry for about 2 minutes.

While the pork is cooking, preheat the grill (broiler) to high. Slice the buns open and place them, cut side up, under the grill for 1 minute, until warmed through and golden.

Meanwhile, warm the cheese in a small saucepan over low heat for 1–2 minutes, until melted.

To assemble, spread the barbecue sauce on the cut sides of the buns. Place the pork strips on the bottom buns, then top with the melted cheese. Sprinkle generously with crispy fried shallots, then the chives. Put the bun lids on top and serve immediately.

HOT TIP!

Add a splash of bourbon
or whisky when cooking
the pork.

HOT TIP!

For extra zing, add some grated lime zest to the yoghurt sauce.

Tandoori chicken BURGERS

a splash of sunflower or vegetable oil

4 x 130 g (4½ oz) boneless, skinless chicken thighs

185 g (6½ oz/¾ cup) tandoori sauce

4 hamburger buns (page 85)

4 teaspoons mango chutney

MINT YOGHURT SAUCE

4 mint leaves, finely chopped

100 g (3½ oz) Greek-style yoghurt

To make the yoghurt sauce, combine the mint leaves and yoghurt and season with salt and pepper.

Heat a little oil in a frying pan over high heat and sear the chicken thighs on both sides. Add the tandoori sauce, turn down the heat and simmer for about 10 minutes, turning the chicken and stirring regularly. Season with salt and pepper.

While the chicken is cooking, preheat the grill (broiler) to high. Slice the buns open and place them, cut side up, under the grill for 1 minute, until warmed through and golden.

To assemble, spread some of the yoghurt sauce on the cut sides of the buns. Place the chicken on the bottom buns and top with the mango chutney. Add the remaining yoghurt sauce, put the bun lids on top and serve immediately.

PERFECT TORTILLAS

The tortilla is the Mexican equivalent of bread. It is made mostly from corn flour, but there is also a wheat-flour version, mainly found in northern Mexico.

Corn was first cultivated in Mexico about 7000 years ago. There are now 64 different varieties in the world, including 59 in Mexico alone, ranging in colour from yellow to purple, blue and even red, each with remarkable nutritional qualities.

To preserve this fantastic biodiversity, consume organic or GMO-free corn whenever possible.

CORN TORTILLAS
MAKES ABOUT 24

1 kg (2 lb 3 oz) masa harina
(ground corn flour)

½ teaspoon salt

2 tablespoons olive oil, plus extra for cooking

500 ml (17 fl oz/2 cups) warm water, approximately

Place the masa harina and salt in a bowl.
Pour in the olive oil and, while mixing, gradually add enough water to make a dough.

Knead the dough until it is firm but springy, adding more water if it's too crumbly.

Divide the dough into small balls. Flatten each ball with a tortilla press or with a rolling pin.

Heat a little oil in a hot frying pan or on a hot griddle and cook the tortillas for 1 minute on each side.

WHEAT TORTILLAS
MAKES 12

400 g (14 oz) plain (all-purpose) flour

a pinch of sugar

a pinch of salt

100 g (3½ oz) butter

olive oil, for cooking

In a bowl, mix together the flour, sugar and salt.
Crumble the butter into the flour. Gradually mix in enough water to make a soft dough.

Divide the dough into 12 even portions and roll into balls. Leave to rest for about 30 minutes.

Using a tortilla press or rolling pin, roll the balls out into discs.

Heat a little oil in a hot frying pan or on a hot griddle and cook the tortillas for 1 minute on each side.

HOT TIP!

You can make these tortillas with purple corn flour (which is rich in antioxidants), or add your favourite herbs.

Essential Tortilla Sauces

Salsa Verde
FOR 4 TACOS

10 tomatillos, or 5 green tomatoes

2 jalapeño chillies

1 garlic clove, roughly chopped

1 tablespoon olive oil

a small handful of coriander (cilantro) leaves

In a large saucepan of boiling water, cook the whole tomatillos and chillies for 10 minutes. Drain and leave to cool slightly. Remove the stems from the chillies.

Transfer the tomatillos and chillies to a blender. Add the garlic and blitz for 2 minutes.

Heat a little oil in a frying pan. Add the tomatillo mixture and cook, stirring occasionally, over medium heat for 10 minutes.

Leave to cool, then chop the coriander and stir it through the salsa.

Salsa Roja
FOR 4 TACOS

5 ripe tomatoes

2 jalapeño chillies

1 garlic clove, roughly chopped

1 tablespoon olive oil

a small handful of coriander (cilantro) leaves

In a large saucepan of boiling water, cook the whole tomatoes and chillies for 10 minutes. Drain and leave to cool slightly. Remove the stems from the chillies.

Transfer the tomatoes and chillies to a blender. Add the garlic and blitz for 2 minutes.

Heat the oil in a frying pan. Add the tomato mixture and cook, stirring occasionally, over medium heat for 10 minutes.

Leave to cool, then chop the coriander and stir it through the salsa.

Pico de Gallo
FOR 4 TACOS

1 mild onion

2 tomatoes

1 jalapeño chilli

a small handful of coriander (cilantro) leaves

juice of 1 lime

Peel and finely dice the onion. Place in a small bowl.

Finely dice the tomatoes and finely chop the chilli. Add them to the onion.

Chop the coriander and mix through the tomato mixture with the lime juice.

GUACAMOLE
FOR 4 TACOS

2 avocados

1 tomato, finely diced

1 jalapeño chilli, finely chopped

a small handful of coriander (cilantro) leaves

juice of 1 lime

Peel the avocados and mash them using a mortar and pestle, or in a bowl with a fork.

Add the tomato and chilli.

Chop the coriander and mix through the avocado mixture with the lime juice.

FRIJOLES
FOR 4 TACOS

100 g (3½ oz) dried red or black beans

1 tablespoon olive oil

1 onion, chopped

1 serrano chilli, or other hot green chilli, finely chopped

a small handful of coriander (cilantro) leaves, chopped

Soak the beans in plenty of cold water overnight, changing the water several times.

Heat the oil in a small frying pan. Add the onion and chilli and sauté over medium heat for about 5 minutes, until the onion has softened.

Add the beans, with about 500 ml (17 fl oz/2 cups) of the soaking water. Increase the heat and allow to boil for 20 minutes. Season with salt and pepper.

Use a potato masher to lightly crush the beans in their own stock. Just before serving, stir the coriander through.

MEXICAN RICE
SERVES 2

1½ tablespoons olive oil

200 g (7 oz/1 cup) long-grain white rice

1 garlic clove, crushed

500 ml (17 fl oz/2 cups) hot chicken stock

125 ml (4 fl oz/½ cup) tomato passata (puréed tomatoes)

½ teaspoon salt

a pinch of ground cumin

Heat the oil in large frying pan over medium heat. Add the rice and cook, stirring often, for 5 minutes, or until golden brown.

Stir in the garlic and fry for 1 minute, then stir in the remaining ingredients. Leave to simmer for 30–40 minutes, or until the rice is tender and there is no liquid remaining.

Fluff the grains up and serve.

HOT TIP!

If you don't have time to soak the dried beans, use tinned beans.

CHICKEN TACOS

MAKES 4

2 boneless, skinless chicken breasts

1 garlic clove, chopped

a handful of coriander (cilantro) leaves, finely chopped

juice of 1 lime

3 tablespoons olive oil

4 corn tortillas (page 145)

4 lettuce leaves

Cut the chicken breasts into small cubes and place them in a bowl. Add the garlic, coriander and lime juice and season with salt and pepper. Mix well. Place in an airtight container and refrigerate for 1 hour.

Heat 2 tablespoons of the oil in a frying pan over medium heat. Add the chicken pieces and cook for about 10 minutes, turning often, until golden brown all over.

Meanwhile, heat the remaining oil in another frying pan and warm the tortillas for 1 minute on each side.

To serve, add a lettuce leaf to each tortilla, then the chicken mixture. Serve immediately, with your choice of accompaniments.

HOT TIP!

Serve with Mexican rice (page 149), Frijoles (page 149) and Pico de gallo (page 146).

BEEF TACOS WITH CAPISCUM

400 g (14 oz) beef fillet

2 tablespoons olive oil

1 onion, thinly sliced

1 green capsicum (bell pepper), thinly sliced

4 corn tortillas (page 145)

thinly sliced radish, to garnish

thinly sliced chilli, to garnish

Cut the beef into small cubes and set aside.

Heat 1 tablespoon of the oil in a frying pan over medium heat. Add the onion and sauté for about 3 minutes. Add the capsicum and beef, season with salt and pepper and sauté for about 15 minutes, until the beef is tender.

Meanwhile, heat the remaining oil in another frying pan and warm the tortillas for 1 minute on each side.

To serve, divide the beef mixture among the tortillas. Garnish with radish and chilli slices and serve immediately, with your choice of accompaniments.

HOT TIP!

Serve with Guacamole (page 149) and Salsa verde (page 146).

CARNITAS TACOS

1 tablespoon olive oil

2 onions, thinly sliced

2 garlic cloves, chopped

1 kg (2 lb 3 oz) pork shoulder

3 x 330–355 ml (11–12 fl oz) bottles of beer (such as Negra Modelo, or your favourite)

1 tablespoon ground cumin

10 coriander seeds

16 corn tortillas (page 145)

thinly sliced red cabbage, to garnish

a small handful of coriander (cilantro) leaves

Preheat the oven to 150°C (300°F).

Heat the oil in a large flameproof casserole dish over medium heat. Add the onion and garlic and sauté for about 3 minutes.

Add the pork shoulder, then pour in the beer, to cover the pork. Add the cumin and coriander seeds and season with salt and pepper. Bring the liquid to a gentle boil, then put the lid on, transfer to the oven and cook for 4 hours.

Remove the pork from the braising liquid, reserving the liquid, and leave the meat until cool enough to handle. Shred the pork, using your hands or a fork.

Preheat the grill (broiler) to medium–high.

Spread the shredded pork and the onion mixture on a baking tray.

Sprinkle with the braising liquid from the casserole dish and place under the grill for 5–10 minutes, to caramelise the pork.

Meanwhile, heat the tortillas in the oven or in a toaster.

To serve, divide the pork and onion mixture among the tortillas. Garnish with red cabbage and coriander leaves and serve immediately, with your choice of accompaniments.

HOT TIP!

Serve with Mexican rice (page 149), Frijoles (page 149) and Pico de gallo (page 146).

Chicken Tinga Tacos

4 garlic cloves, peeled

1 whole free-range chicken

3 onions, peeled

2 tablespoons olive oil

2 x 400 g (14 oz) tins of chopped tomatoes

200 (7 oz) tin of chipotle chillies in adobo sauce

12 corn tortillas (page 145)

150 g (5½ oz) queso fresco, or other soft white fresh cheese, crumbled or grated

a small handful of coriander (cilantro) leaves, chopped

thinly sliced radish, to garnish

Preheat the oven to 200°C (400°F).

Cut two garlic cloves in half. Rub the cut side of two of the garlic halves all over the chicken and discard. Place the other two garlic cloves inside the chicken. Cut one onion in half or into quarters and also place inside the chicken.

Place the chicken in a large baking dish and bake for 1½ hours, basting at least twice.

Remove the chicken from the oven and leave until cool enough to handle. Shred the meat coarsely.

Heat the oil in a large flameproof casserole dish over medium heat. Chop the remaining two onions and garlic cloves and sauté for 5 minutes, until soft and golden.

Place the tomatoes and chipotle chillies (and their adobo sauce) in a blender and blitz for a few seconds, until smooth. Add the sauce to the casserole, along with the shredded chicken, stirring well. Season with salt and pepper and simmer over low heat for 1 hour.

Just before serving, heat the tortillas in a hot frying pan.

To serve, divide the chicken mixture among the tortillas. Sprinkle with the cheese and coriander, garnish with radish and serve immediately, with your choice of accompaniments.

HOT TIP!

Serve with Salsa roja (page 146) and Guacamole (page 149).

BEEF & RED BEAN TACOS

2 ripe tomatoes

1 tablespoon olive oil

1 onion, thinly sliced

1 garlic clove, finely chopped

200 g (7 oz) minced (ground) beef

4 tablespoons tinned red beans, rinsed and drained

4 wheat tortillas (page 145)

a handful of grated cheddar or monterey jack

a small handful of coriander (cilantro) leaves, chopped

Plunge the tomatoes into a saucepan of boiling water for 2 minutes. Drain and leave to cool slightly, then peel them. Finely dice and set aside.

Heat the oil in a small saucepan over medium heat. Sauté the onion and garlic for 2 minutes, then stir in the diced tomato and the beef, breaking up any bigger lumps of meat.

Add the beans, season with salt and pepper and mix together well. Cook over low heat for 10 minutes.

Meanwhile, heat the tortillas in the oven or in a toaster.

To serve, divide the beef mixture among the tortillas. Sprinkle with the grated cheese and coriander and serve immediately, with your choice of accompaniments.

HOT TIP!

Serve with Mexican rice (page 149) and Salsa roja (page 146).

Tacos with Chorizo & Potato

4 potatoes

2 tablespoons olive oil

1 onion, thinly sliced

1 chorizo sausage, cut into small chunks

8 corn tortillas (page 145)

juice of ½ lime

Peel the potatoes and cut into chunks. Add them to a saucepan of salted boiling water and cook for 10–15 minutes, or until tender.

Meanwhile, heat 1 tablespoon of the oil in a frying pan over medium heat. Sauté the onion and chorizo for about 5 minutes, until nicely browned.

When the potatoes are cooked, drain well, then mash with a fork. Add the chorizo and onion and season with salt and pepper. Keep warm.

Heat the remaining oil in another frying pan and warm the tortillas for 1 minute on each side.

To serve, divide the chorizo mixture among the tortillas. Sprinkle with the lime juice and serve immediately, with your choice of accompaniments.

HOT TIP!

Serve with Pico de gallo (page 146).

CHICKEN FAJITA TACOS

2 tablespoons olive oil

2 boneless, skinless chicken breasts, thinly sliced

1 large onion, thinly sliced

1 red capsicum (bell pepper), thinly sliced

4 wheat tortillas (page 145)

Guacamole (page 149), to serve

Heat the oil in a frying pan over medium heat. Sauté the chicken, onion and capsicum for 15 minutes, or until the onion is caramelised and the chicken is browned all over. Season with salt and pepper.

Just before serving, heat the tortillas in the oven or in a toaster.

Divide the chicken mixture among the tortillas. Add the guacamole and serve immediately.

CARNE ASADA TACOS

1 onion, finely chopped

2 jalapeño chillies, finely chopped

1 garlic clove, finely chopped

a small handful of coriander (cilantro) leaves, finely chopped

juice of 4 limes

4 tablespoons olive oil

400 g (14 oz) beef fillet

4 corn tortillas (page 145)

a handful of shredded lettuce, to serve

Combine the onion, chilli, garlic and coriander in a bowl. Stir in the lime juice and most of the oil and season with salt and pepper. Add the beef, turning to coat. Cover with plastic wrap and marinate in the refrigerator for at least 1 hour, or up to 6 hours.

Remove the beef from the marinade. Place in a hot frying pan or on a hot griddle and cook for a few minutes on each side. Leave to cool slightly, then cut the meat into thin strips.

Meanwhile, heat the remaining oil in another frying pan and warm the tortillas for 1 minute on each side.

To serve, add some lettuce to each tortillas. Top with the beef and serve immediately, with your choice of accompaniments.

HOT TIP!

Serve with Mexican rice (page 149), Frijoles (page 149) and Pico de gallo (page 146).

Tacos al Pastor

4 tomatoes

2 serrano chillies, or other hot green chillies

2 garlic cloves, roughly chopped

250 ml (8½ fl oz/1 cup) fresh pineapple juice

1 kg (2 lb 3 oz) pork loin, cut into chunks

3 tablespoons olive oil

2 onions, thinly sliced

1 pineapple, finely chopped

16 purple corn tortillas (page 145)

juice of 1 lime

a small handful of coriander (cilantro) leaves

In a large saucepan of boiling water, cook the whole tomatoes and chillies for 10 minutes. Drain and leave to cool slightly. Remove the stems from the chillies.

Put the tomatoes and chillies in a blender. Add one of the garlic cloves and the pineapple juice and blend until smooth. Season with salt.

Put the pork in a bowl, then cover with the marinade, tossing to coat. Cover with plastic wrap and marinate in the refrigerator for at least 30 minutes.

Heat the oil in a large flameproof casserole dish over medium heat. Add the onion and remaining garlic and sauté for about 5 minutes.

Add the pork and the marinade, stirring well. Cover and simmer over low heat for at least 1 hour, until the pork is tender.

Remove from the heat and leave until cool enough to handle, then finely shred the pork, into a bowl. Mix the pineapple through.

Heat a splash of oil in a frying pan and warm the tortillas for 1 minute on each side.

To serve, divide the pork mixture among the tortillas. Sprinkle with the lime juice, scatter with coriander and serve immediately, with your choice of accompaniments.

HOT TIP!

Serve with Mexican rice (page 149), Frijoles (page 149) and Salsa roja (page 146).

FISH TACOS

juice of 1 lime

1 garlic clove, finely chopped

400 g (14 oz) firm white fish fillets, skin removed

2 potatoes, peeled and cut into chunks

3 tablespoons olive oil

4 corn tortillas (page 145)

Combine the lime juice and garlic in a bowl. Add the fish fillets, turning to coat. Cover with plastic wrap and marinate in the refrigerator for about 1 hour.

Add the potato chunks to a saucepan of salted boiling water and cook for 10–15 minutes, or until tender. Drain, then place in a small bowl. Add 1 tablespoon of the oil, season with salt and pepper and mash with a fork. Set aside and keep warm.

Heat a splash of oil in a frying pan or griddle over medium heat. Add the fish and grill for a few minutes on each side, until just cooked through. Flake into chunks.

Meanwhile, heat the remaining oil in another frying pan and warm the tortillas for 1 minute on each side.

To serve, spread a spoonful of mashed potato onto each tortilla. Add the fish and serve immediately, with your choice of accompaniments.

HOT TIP!

Serve with Pico de gallo (page 146) and Salsa verde (page 146).

CEVICHE TACOS WITH MANGO

400 g (14 oz) very fresh firm white fish fillets, skin removed

1 onion

1 serrano chilli, or other hot green chilli

½ mango

juice of 1 lime

juice of 1 orange

4 purple corn tortillas (page 145)

a small handful of coriander (cilantro) leaves, chopped

Cut the fish into small chunks.

Finely chop the onion and chilli and place in a bowl. Cut the mango flesh into small chunks and add to the bowl, along with the lime juice and orange juice. Mix together and season with salt and pepper.

Add the fish, turning to coat. Cover with plastic wrap and marinate in the refrigerator for about 30 minutes, but no longer than 1 hour.

Just before serving, heat the tortillas in the oven or in a toaster.

To serve, divide the fish mixture among the tortillas. Scatter with the coriander and serve immediately, with your choice of accompaniments.

HOT TIP!

Serve with Mexican rice (page 149).

SALMON TACOS

juice of 2 limes

250 ml (8½ fl oz/1 cup) fresh pineapple juice

2 cm (¾ in) knob of fresh ginger, peeled and grated

handful of coriander (cilantro) leaves, finely chopped

400 g (14 oz) salmon fillets, skin and pin bones removed

1 tablespoon olive oil

4 corn tortillas (page 145)

Pour the lime juice and pineapple juice into a bowl. Stir in the ginger and coriander and season with salt and pepper.

Add the salmon fillets, turning to coat. Cover with plastic wrap and marinate in the refrigerator for about 1 hour.

Preheat the oven to 200°C (400°F). Place the salmon fillets on a baking tray lined with baking paper and bake for 15 minutes.

Meanwhile, heat the oil in a frying pan and warm the tortillas for 1 minute on each side.

To serve, flake the salmon with a fork and divide among the tortillas. Serve immediately, with your choice of accompaniments.

HOT TIP!

Serve with Guacamole (page 149) and Pico de gallo (page 146).

CHILLI PRAWN TACOS

16 raw prawns (shrimp), peeled and deveined

juice of 4 limes

2 serrano chillies, or other hot green chillies, chopped

1 tablespoon olive oil

4 corn tortillas (page 145)

Place the prawns in a bowl with the lime juice and chilli. Season with salt and pepper and mix together. Cover with plastic wrap and marinate in the refrigerator for about 1 hour.

Heat the oil in a frying pan or griddle over medium heat. Add the prawns and cook for about 1 minute on each side, until just cooked through.

Meanwhile, heat a splash of oil in another frying pan and warm the tortillas for 1 minute on each side.

Divide the prawns among the tortillas and serve immediately, with your choice of accompaniments.

HOT TIP!

Serve with Guacamole (page 149) and Pico de gallo (page 146).

Asparagus & Cheese Tacos

4 tomatoes

3 tablespoons olive oil

1 onion, thinly sliced

1 serrano chilli, or other hot green chilli, thinly sliced

16 asparagus spears, stalks trimmed

4 purple corn tortillas (page 145)

4 tablespoons crumbled or grated queso fresco, or other soft white fresh cheese

Plunge the tomatoes into a saucepan of boiling water for 2 minutes. Drain and leave to cool slightly, then peel them. Finely dice and set aside.

Heat 2 tablespoons of the oil in a frying pan over medium heat. Sauté the onion for about 5 minutes, then stir in the chilli and diced tomatoes. Season with salt and pepper, then cover and simmer for 5–10 minutes. Transfer to a bowl and leave to cool.

Meanwhile, soak the asparagus spears in a bowl of cold water for 10 minutes. Drain well.

Preheat the grill (broiler) to medium–high.

Brown the asparagus under the grill for about 4 minutes, turning now and then, until slightly softened.

Meanwhile, heat the remaining oil in a frying pan and warm the tortillas for 1 minute on each side.

To serve, divide the asparagus among the tortillas. Top with the cheese and the tomato sauce and serve immediately, with your choice of accompaniments.

HOT TIP!

Serve with Guacamole (page 149).

CREAMY JALAPEÑO MASHED POTATO TACOS

4 large potatoes

2 tablespoons crema Mexicana or fresh cream

2 tablespoons grated mozzarella

3 tablespoons olive oil

1 onion, thinly sliced

1 jalapeño chilli, thinly sliced

4 purple corn tortillas (page 145)

Peel the potatoes and cut into chunks. Add to a saucepan of salted boiling water and cook for 10–15 minutes, or until tender.

Drain the potatoes, then place in a bowl. Add the cream and cheese and mash together, using a fork.

Heat 2 tablespoons of the oil in a frying pan over medium heat. Sauté the onion and chilli for about 5 minutes, then stir the mixture through the mashed potato. Keep warm.

Heat the remaining oil in a frying pan and warm the tortillas for 1 minute on each side.

Spread the mashed potato mixture over the tortillas and serve immediately, with your choice of accompaniments.

HOT TIP!

Serve with Salsa verde (page 146).

179

200 g (7 oz/1 cup) puy lentils or tiny blue-green lentils

3 tablespoons olive oil

1 onion, thinly sliced

1 green capsicum (bell pepper), thinly sliced

4 corn tortillas (page 145)

a small handful of coriander (cilantro) leaves, chopped

Cook the lentils in a saucepan of boiling salted water for 15–25 minutes, until tender. Drain and set aside.

Meanwhile, heat 2 tablespoons of the oil in a frying pan over medium heat. Sauté the onion and capsicum for about 10 minutes.

Stir in the lentils, season with salt and pepper and cook for a minute or two, until the lentils are warmed through.

Heat the remaining oil in another frying pan and warm the tortillas for 1 minute on each side.

Divide the lentil mixture among the tortillas, scatter with the coriander and serve immediately, with your choice of accompaniments.

HOT TIP!

Serve with Guacamole (page 149) and Salsa roja (page 146).

ROASTED WINTER VEGIE TACOS

1 carrot, peeled

1 small sweet potato, peeled

1 turnip, peeled

1 parsnip, peeled

1 celery stalk, finely chopped

1 onion, thinly sliced

3 tablespoons olive oil, plus extra for drizzling

1 small red cabbage

juice of 2 limes

a small handful of coriander (cilantro) leaves, chopped

8 corn tortillas (page 145)

4 tablespoons fresh goat's cheese

Preheat the oven to 200°C (400°F).

Cut the carrot, sweet potato, turnip and parsnip into small cubes. Arrange on a baking tray with the celery and onion. Drizzle with a splash of oil and season with salt and pepper. Roast for 30–40 minutes, until the vegetables are tender, turning now and then.

Meanwhile, shred the cabbage and place in a large bowl. Add the lime juice, coriander and 2 tablespoons of the oil. Season with salt and pepper and toss together. Cover and set aside for at least 15 minutes.

Just before serving, heat the remaining oil in another frying pan and warm the tortillas for 1 minute on each side.

Divide the roasted vegetables among the tortillas. Top with some of the cabbage, then the goat's cheese, and serve immediately.

VEGETABLE QUESADILLAS

MAKES 2

3 tablespoons olive oil

1 onion, finely chopped

4 mushrooms, finely chopped

1 small zucchini (courgette), thinly sliced

100 g (3½ oz) grated mozzarella

2 large wheat tortillas (page 145)

Heat 2 tablespoons of the oil in a frying pan over medium heat. Sauté the onion, mushrooms and zucchini for about 10 minutes, until tender. Season with salt and pepper.

Heat the remaining oil in another frying pan over medium heat. Add one of the tortillas, and arrange half the cheese and half the cooked vegetables on one side. Close the tortilla into a half-moon and cook for 1 minute on each side. Remove from the pan and keep warm.

Repeat with the remaining tortilla, cheese and vegetable mixture.

Cut each tortilla into wedges and serve immediately, with your choice of accompaniments.

HOT TIP!

Serve with Guacamole (page 149) and Salsa verde (page 146).

Bean & Roasted Pumpkin Tostadas

1 small pumpkin (winter squash)

1 green capsicum (bell pepper), thinly sliced

1 serrano chilli, or other hot green chilli, sliced

olive oil, for drizzling and brushing

4 corn tortillas (page 145)

4 tablespoons Frijoles (page 149)

4 tablespoons crumbled queso fresco or feta

a small handful of coriander (cilantro) leaves, chopped

Preheat the oven to 200°C (400°F).

Peel the pumpkin and remove the seeds. Cut into small cubes and arrange on a baking tray with the capsicum and chilli. Drizzle with a splash of oil and season with salt and pepper.

Roast for 25–30 minutes, until the pumpkin is tender, turning now and then. Remove from the oven and leave to cool slightly, leaving the oven on.

Lightly brush a little olive oil over both sides of each tortilla. Place them on an oven rack and toast them in the oven for about 5 minutes.

To serve, spread the frijoles over each tortilla. Top with the roasted pumpkin, cheese and coriander and serve immediately, with your choice of accompaniments.

HOT TIP!

Serve with Guacamole (page 149) and Salsa verde (page 146).

Sweet Tacos

Flambéed Mango Tacos
MAKES 4

1 ripe mango
1 tablespoon butter
60 ml (2 fl oz/¼ cup) tequila
4 corn tortillas (page 145)

Peel the mango and cut the flesh into thin slices.

Melt half the butter in a frying pan, then arrange the mango slices around the pan. Pour in the tequila and very carefully set it alight, to flambé the mango. Allow the flame to extinguish itself, then set aside.

In another frying pan, melt the remaining butter and heat the tortillas for 1 minute on each side.

Spread the flambéed mango over each tortilla and serve immediately.

Caramelised Banana Tacos
MAKES 4

2 bananas
1 tablespoon butter
sugar, for sprinkling
4 corn tortillas (page 145)

Peel the bananas and cut into thin slices.

Melt half the butter in a frying pan, arrange the banana slices around the pan and sprinkle them with sugar. Cook over medium heat for 5–10 minutes, until caramelised.

In another frying pan, melt the remaining butter and heat the tortillas for 1 minute on each side.

Spread the caramelised banana over each tortilla and serve immediately.

Papaya & Cocoa Tacos
MAKES 4

½ papaya
4 corn tortillas (page 145)
4 tablespoons unsweetened cocoa powder

Peel the papaya and cut into small cubes. Divide among the tortillas, sprinkle with the cocoa powder and serve immediately.

HOT TIP!

Serve the fruit tacos with a scoop of vanilla ice cream.

Classic Margarita

80 ml (2½ fl oz) tequila

40 ml (1¼ fl oz) triple sec
or Cointreau

60 ml (2 fl oz) lime juice

40 ml (1¼ fl oz) orange juice

20 ml (¾ fl oz) raw cane
sugar syrup (see Hot tips!)

ice cubes

½ lemon

coarse salt or sea salt

Add the tequila, triple sec, lime juice, orange juice and sugar syrup to a cocktail shaker. Shake with plenty of ice cubes for about 30 seconds, until chilled.

Run the lemon over the rim of two chilled margarita glasses. Spread some salt on a plate and dip the glass rims in, to crust with salt.

Strain the margarita mix into the glasses and serve.

HOT TIPS!

To make raw cane sugar syrup, gently heat one part water and two parts raw cane sugar in a saucepan, stirring to dissolve the sugar. Remove from the heat immediately, before the sugar caramelises.

For a colourful touch, add some food colouring to the salt you use to rim the margarita glasses!

Margarita 'on the rocks'

Place 4 ice cubes in the bottom of each glass before adding the margarita mix.

Frozen Margarita

Put the margarita ingredients in a blender with a handful of ice cubes and blitz for a few seconds before serving.

BLUEBERRY
MAKES 2

125 g (4½ oz) blueberries

20 ml (¾ fl oz) raw cane sugar syrup (page 191)

1 lime, cut in half

80 ml (2½ fl oz) tequila

40 ml (1¼ fl oz) triple sec or Cointreau

ice cubes

coarse salt or sea salt

Place the berries in a saucepan with 200 ml (7 fl oz) water and the sugar syrup. Add the juice from the lime, reserving the lime halves. Bring to a gentle boil, stirring to dissolve the sugar. Leave to cool, then strain the syrup.

Pour 200 ml (7 fl oz) of the blueberry syrup into a blender. Add the tequila, triple sec and a large handful of ice cubes and blitz until combined.

Rub the reserved lime halves over the rim of two chilled margarita glasses, then dip the rims in a saucer of salt.

Pour the margarita mix into the glasses and serve.

STRAWBERRY
MAKES 2

250 g (9 oz) strawberries, hulled

80 ml (2½ fl oz) tequila

40 ml (1¼ fl oz) triple sec or Cointreau

ice cubes

½ lime

coarse salt or sea salt

Put the strawberries in a blender. Add the tequila, triple sec and a large handful of ice cubes and blitz until combined.

Rub the lime half over the rim of two chilled margarita glasses, then dip the rims in a saucer of salt.

Pour the margarita mix into the glasses and serve.

RASPBERRY
MAKES 2

125 g (4½ oz) raspberries

80 ml (2½ fl oz) tequila

40 ml (1¼ fl oz) triple sec or Cointreau

ice cubes

½ lime

coarse salt or sea salt

Put the raspberries in a blender. Add the tequila, triple sec and a large handful of ice cubes and blitz until combined.

Rub the lime half over the rim of two chilled margarita glasses, then dip the rims in a saucer of salt.

Pour the margarita mix into the glasses and serve.

HOT TIP!

Instead of blending the margaritas with ice cubes, combine the ingredients in a cocktail shaker full of ice and shake until chilled, then serve over ice.

TROPICAL MARGARITAS

PASSIONFRUIT
MAKES 2

10 passionfruit, cut in half

200 ml (7 fl oz) water

1 tablespoon raw sugar

1 lime, cut in half

80 ml (2½ fl oz) tequila

40 ml (1¼ fl oz) triple sec or Cointreau

ice cubes and crushed ice

coarse salt or sea salt

Scoop the passionfruit pulp into a saucepan with 200 ml (7 fl oz) water. Add the sugar and the juice from the lime, reserving the lime halves. Bring to a gentle boil, stirring to dissolve the sugar. Leave to cool, then strain the syrup.

Pour 200 ml (7 fl oz) of the passionfruit syrup into a cocktail shaker. Add the tequila, triple sec and a handful of ice cubes and shake for about 30 seconds, until chilled.

Rub the reserved lime halves over the rim of two chilled margarita glasses, then dip the rims in a saucer of salt. Fill with crushed ice.

Strain the margarita mix into the glasses and serve.

MANGO & ORANGE
MAKES 2

1 mango, flesh roughly chopped

1 seedless orange, flesh roughly chopped

80 ml (2½ fl oz) tequila

40 ml (1¼ fl oz) triple sec or cointreau

½ lime

coarse salt or sea salt

crushed ice

Put the mango and orange in a blender. Add the tequila and triple sec and blend for 1 minute.

Rub the lime half over the rim of two chilled margarita glasses, then dip the rims in a saucer of salt. Fill with crushed ice.

Pour the margarita mix into the glasses and serve.

PINEAPPLE
MAKES 2

1 small pineapple, peeled and diced

juice of 1 lemon

20 ml (¾ fl oz) raw cane sugar syrup (page 191)

80 ml (2½ fl oz) tequila

40 ml (1¼ fl oz) triple sec or Cointreau

½ lime

coarse salt or sea salt

crushed ice

Put the pineapple and lemon juice in a blender. Add the sugar syrup and blend for 1 minute. Add the tequila and triple sec and blend again.

Rub the lime half over the rim of two chilled margarita glasses, then dip the rims in a saucer of salt. Fill with crushed ice.

Pour the margarita mix into the glasses and serve.

FROZEN MARGARITAS

Put the margarita ingredients in a blender with a large handful of ice cubes and blitz for a few seconds before serving.

Watermelon
MAKES 2

½ watermelon

80 ml (2½ fl oz) tequila

40 ml (1¼ fl oz) triple sec
or Cointreau

½ lime

coarse salt or sea salt

crushed ice

Remove the peel from the watermelon and cut the flesh into chunks, discarding the seeds. Place in a blender, add the tequila and triple sec and blend until combined. Strain to remove any last seeds.

Rub the lime half over the rim of two chilled margarita glasses, then dip the rims in a saucer of salt. Fill with crushed ice.

Pour the margarita mix into the glasses and serve.

Peach
MAKES 2

3 peaches

80 ml (2½ fl oz) tequila

40 ml (1¼ fl oz) triple sec
or cointreau

½ lime

coarse salt or sea salt

crushed ice

Peel the peaches, remove the stones and cut the flesh into chunks. Place in a blender, add the tequila and triple sec and blend until combined.

Rub the lime half over the rim of two chilled margarita glasses, then dip the rims in a saucer of salt. Fill with crushed ice.

Pour the margarita mix into the glasses and serve.

Melon
MAKES 2

1 melon of your choice

80 ml (2½ fl oz) tequila

40 ml (1¼ fl oz) triple sec
or Cointreau

½ lime

coarse salt or sea salt

crushed ice

Remove the peel from the melon and cut the flesh into chunks, discarding the seeds. Place in a blender, add the tequila and triple sec and blend until combined. Strain to remove any last seeds.

Rub the lime half over the rim of two chilled margarita glasses, then dip the rims in a saucer of salt. Fill with crushed ice.

Pour the margarita mix into the glasses and serve.

Frozen Margarita

Put the margarita ingredients in a blender with a large handful of ice cubes and blitz for a few seconds before serving.

TEQUILA
COCKTAILS

TEQUILA SUNRISE
MAKES 1

ice cubes

60 ml (2 fl oz) tequila

120 ml (4 fl oz) orange juice

20 ml (¾ fl oz) grenadine

Place some ice cubes in the bottom of a chilled margarita glass.

Slowly pour in the tequila, then the orange juice, then the grenadine, and serve.

MEXICO LINDO
MAKES 2

60 ml (2 fl oz) tequila

120 ml (4 fl oz) curaçao

60 ml (2 fl oz) lime juice

ice cubes

2–4 pitted cherries

Add the tequila, curaçao and lime juice to a cocktail shaker. Shake with plenty of ice cubes for about 30 seconds, until chilled.

Pour into two chilled margarita glasses and garnish with cherries.

PALOMA
MAKES 1

40 ml (1¼ fl oz) tequila

20 ml (¾ fl oz) lime juice

a pinch of salt

ice cubes

120 ml (4 fl oz) grapefruit juice

lime slices, to garnish

Pour the tequila and lime juice into a chilled margarita glass. Add a pinch of salt.

Add some ice cubes, then the grapefruit juice. Mix with a spoon and garnish with lime slices.

Beer with a Shot of Tequila
MAKES 1

40 ml (1¼ fl oz) tequila

1 x 355 ml (12 fl oz) bottle
of Mexican beer

a pinch of salt

a wedge of lime or lemon

Pour the tequila into a shot glass.

Serve with the beer, with a pinch of
salt and a citrus wedge to chew on.

The Submarine
MAKES 1

40 ml (1¼ fl oz) aged
amber tequila

1 x 355 ml (12 fl oz) bottle
of Mexican beer

a pinch of salt

a wedge of lime or lemon

Pour the tequila into a shot glass.

Put the shot glass, upside down, in
the bottom of a large beer glass.

Pour in the beer and serve with a
pinch of salt and a citrus wedge.

The Cockroach
MAKES 1

20 ml (¾ fl oz) Kahlúa

40 ml (1¼ fl oz) tequila

Pour the Kahlúa into a shot glass.
Gently add the tequila.

Carefully ignite the tequila with
a lighter. You have 5 seconds to
plant a straw into the shot glass
and drink your treat!

Mezcal Cocktails

The Matador
MAKES 1

¼ pineapple, peeled and diced
60 ml (2 fl oz) white mezcal
2 tablespoons lime juice
ice cubes

Put the pineapple in a blender
and blitz until juiced.

Pour 100 ml (3½ fl oz) of the
pineapple juice into a cocktail shaker.
Add the mezcal, lime juice and a
handful of ice cubes and shake for
about 30 seconds, until chilled.

Strain into a chilled glass and serve.

Mexico Pacifico
MAKES 1

60 ml (2 fl oz) white mezcal
juice of 1 lime
40 ml (1¼ fl oz) grenadine
ice cubes

Pour the mezcal, lime juice
and grenadine into a blender.
Add lots of ice cubes and blend
for 1 minute.

Pour into a chilled glass and serve.

Hot Chocolate with Mezcal
MAKES 2

500 ml (17 fl oz/2 cups) milk
30 g (1 oz/¼ cup) unsweetened
cocoa powder
1 teaspoon purple corn
flour (maize flour)
1 tablespoon honey
1 dried chilli
150 ml (5 fl oz) white mezcal

Pour the milk into a saucepan.
Add the cocoa powder, corn flour,
honey and chilli and heat gently
for about 10 minutes, mixing well.

Pass the mixture through a
strainer, to remove the chilli and
any seeds that may have been
released into the milk.

Place back over low heat and add
the mezcal, stirring for about
1 minute to heat through.

Pour into two cups and serve.

ADELITA
MAKES 1

100 ml (3½ fl oz) tequila

20 ml (¾ fl oz) Kahlúa

juice of ½ lime

ice cubes

Pour the tequila, Kahlúa and lime juice into a cocktail shaker. Add a few ice cubes and shake for about 30 seconds, until chilled.

Strain into a chilled martini glass and serve.

KAHLÚA COLADA
MAKES 1

60 ml (2 fl oz) Kahlúa

60 ml (2 fl oz) milk

30 ml (1 fl oz) coconut milk

ice cubes

Place the Kahlúa, milk and coconut milk in a blender. Add some ice cubes and blend for a few seconds.

Pour into a chilled martini glass and serve.

BLACK RUSSIAN
MAKES 1

ice cubes

60 ml (2 fl oz) vodka

30 ml (1 fl oz) Kahlúa

1 glacé cherry

Chill a martini glass in the freezer for about 10 minutes.

Fill the martini glass with ice cubes. Pour in the vodka, then the Kahlúa, and stir vigorously for 3 seconds.

Garnish with the glacé cherry and serve.

ESPRESSO MARTINI
MAKES 1

45 ml (1½ fl oz) Kahlúa

30 ml (1 fl oz) vodka

45 ml (1½ fl oz) chilled espresso coffee

ice cubes

Pour the Kahlúa, vodka and coffee into a cocktail shaker. Add a few ice cubes and shake for about 30 seconds, until chilled.

Strain into a chilled martini glass and serve.

Beer Cocktails

MICHELADA
MAKES 1

1 x 355 ml (12 fl oz) bottle of Mexican beer

1 lime, cut in half

coarse salt or sea salt

ice cubes

a dash of worcestershire sauce

Place a beer glass and your bottle of beer in the freezer for a few minutes.

Rub half a lime over the rim of the glass, then dip the rim in a saucer of salt.

Add the juice from the lime and a few ice cubes, then pour in the beer. Add a dash of worcestershire sauce and serve.

CHELADA
MAKES 1

1 x 355 ml (12 fl oz) bottle of Mexican beer

2 limes, cut in half

coarse salt or sea salt

ice cubes

Place a large beer glass and your bottle of beer in the freezer for a few minutes.

Rub half a lime over the rim of the glass, then dip the rim in a saucer of salt.

Pour in the juice from the limes, then the beer. Add a few ice cubes and serve.

LA ENDIABLADA
MAKES 1

2 limes, cut in half

coarse salt or sea salt

ice cubes

30 ml (1 fl oz) tequila

a dash of Tabasco or other hot chilli sauce

1 x 355 ml (12 fl oz) bottle of Mexican beer

Rub half a lime over the rim of a large beer glass, then dip the rim in a saucer of salt. Add some ice cubes to the glass.

Pour in the tequila, then add the juice from the limes, and a dash of Tabasco.

Pour in the beer and serve.

Exotic
Infusions

HIBISCUS TISANE
SERVES 8

2 teaspoons raw cane
sugar syrup (page 191; optional)
1 cup dried hibiscus flowers
1 litre (34 fl oz/4 cups) chilled water
1 lime, thinly sliced (optional)
ice cubes

Bring 1 litre (34 fl oz/4 cups)
water to the boil in a saucepan,
with the sugar if you'd like a
sweeter infusion, or without if
you'd like it sugar-free.

Put the hibiscus flowers in a
large heatproof jug and pour the
boiling water over them. Allow to
infuse for about 20 minutes.

Remove the hibiscus flowers and
add the chilled water.

Add the lime slices if desired.
Serve in cold glasses over ice.

TAMARIND TISANE
SERVES 4

15 whole tamarind pods
1½ tablespoons sugar, or to taste
ice cubes

Bring 1 litre (34 fl oz/4 cups) water
to the boil in a saucepan.

Meanwhile, remove and discard the
outer shell of the tamarind pods.

When the water boils, remove
from the heat and add the tamarind
seeds and sugar. Stir to dissolve the
sugar, then leave to soak for
about 1½ hours.

Use your fingers to remove the
hard black seeds.

Place the liquid and remaining pulp
in a blender and whiz until the pulp
is completely puréed and combined.

Pass the liquid through a strainer
to remove the excess pulp.

Refrigerate for a few hours and
serve in cold glasses over ice.

Mocktails

MANGO & PINEAPPLE SMOOTHIE
SERVES 4

1 pineapple, flesh diced
1 mango, flesh diced
300 ml (10 fl oz) rice milk
ice cubes or crushed ice

Place the pineapple, mango and rice milk in a blender. Whiz until well combined.

Pour into a jug quarter-filled with ice cubes or crushed ice.

Stir and serve.

WATERMELON & MINT JUICE
SERVES 4

1 watermelon
ice cubes
10 mint leaves

Remove the peel from the watermelon and cut the flesh into chunks, discarding the seeds. Place in a blender and whiz to a purée. Strain to remove any last seeds.

Pour the watermelon juice into a jug containing plenty of ice cubes.

Stir in the mint leaves and serve.

BERRY SMOOTHIE
SERVES 2

125 g (4½ oz) fresh raspberries
125 g (4½ oz) fresh blackberries
125 g (4½ oz) fresh blueberries
300 ml (10 fl oz) almond milk
ice cubes

Wash all the berries well and place in a blender.

Add the almond milk and a handful of ice cubes and blend for a few seconds.

Pour into large glasses and enjoy without moderation – berries are full of antioxidants!

Index

Published in 2018 by Smith Street Books
Melbourne • Australia | smithstreetbooks.com

ISBN: 978-1-925418-49-1

CIP data is available from the National Library of Australia

Publisher: Paul McNally
Project editor: Hannah Koelmeyer
Editor: Katri Hilden
Design, layout & illustration: Stephanie Spartels

Photographer: pages 9–140 Charlotte Lascève, pages 144–210 David Japy

Printed & bound in China by C&C Offset Printing Co., Ltd.

Book 55
10 9 8 7 6 5 4 3 2 1